THE BILL

THE iNSiDE STORY

Rachel Silver has written for television and the national press. She worked for several years as a drama script editor, and has since published six books, including three television tie-ins. Most recently she has written *Madson*, a novel based on the BBC police drama, and *Casualty: Behind the Scenes* for BBC Books. Rachel lives in west London with her son José.

Acknowledgements
The author and publishers are grateful to Gary Sleeman, Richard Handford and Julie Dixon, to Nuala Giblin and Rosane Davis at The Bill press office, to scheduler Nigel Wilson who is central to all action at The Bill, to Pat Smith at Carlton Television, Elizabeth Jones and Paul Stevens at ICM, Robert Gwyn Palmer at Pearson Television and all members of the cast and crew at The Bill for their valuable and generous advice.

Thanks also to Pat Dyos, Simon Farrell and Tony Russell for photographic material.

THE BILL
THE iNSiDE STORY
BEHiND THE SCENES OF BRiTAiN'S TOP POLICE DRAMA

RACHEL SiLVER

HarperCollins*Entertainment*
An Imprint of HarperCollins*Publishers*

HarperCollins*Entertainment*
An Imprint of HarperCollins*Publishers*
77–85 Fulham Palace Road,
Hammersmith, London W6 8JB

www.**fire**and**water**.com

Published by HarperCollins*Publishers* 1999
1 2 3 4 5 6 7 8 9

Based on the Thames Television series The Bill,
devised by Geoff McQueen

A catalogue record for this book
is available from the British Library

ISBN 0 00 257137 4

Set in Gill Sans

Designed by Design Principals, Warminster

Printed and bound in Great Britain by
Scotprint, Musselburgh, Scotland

Visit The Bill's official website:
http://www.thebill.com/

Contents

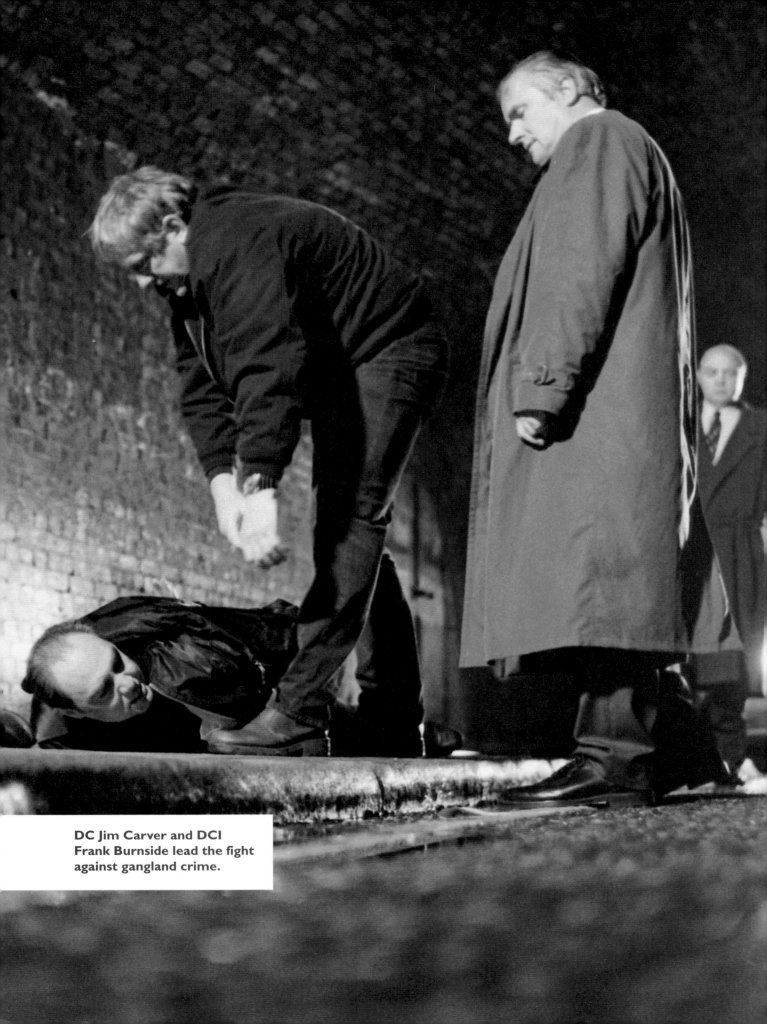

DC Jim Carver and DCI Frank Burnside lead the fight against gangland crime.

With its gripping plots and vibrant authenticity, The Bill is the most successful police drama series on British television ever. It has run for over fifteen years, moving from its original hourly slot to a twice-weekly half-hour format in 1988, to three times a week in 1993 and then back to the orginal one-hour episodes by popular request in summer 1998. The programme thrives on a hard-hitting, provocative and compelling blend of realistic stories and characters that entertain an audience of millions.

The Bill's warehouse offices – called Bosun House, after a former executive producer's dog that became the staff mascot – are situated on a south London industrial estate. From there, Thames Television currently makes almost a hundred episodes a year, and employs an astonishing 240 people permanently on site. The world of The Bill is a unique hub of activity where fiction and reality blur as the vast team work in perfect synchronicity to create the twice weekly dramas that we know as Sun Hill.

On the approach to Bosun House a police car screeches round the corner. Is it real, or is it a high speed chase caught on camera for another episode of The Bill? Inside the building actors in uniform wander the corridors. Outside the photocopying room Christopher Ellison, alias DCI Frank Burnside, talks earnestly into a mobile phone. Between takes senior officers wearing the customary rumpled suits of CID and thick TV make-up sit in the canteen over cups of tea. In the press office Samantha Robson, who plays PC Hagen, pores over a photo spread she has recently done for the men's magazine Loaded. It is a

The experienced PC Stamp takes the novice Ashton under his wing.

surreal landscape in which anything feels possible, and you never know who or what might be around the corner.

Drawn into the heart of the production process, the sheer scale of the enterprise rapidly becomes apparent. The Bill team are responsible for two hours of prime-time television drama per week on a regular

When a driver plunges headlong into a river and PC Santini is first on the scene, it proves to be a complex scene for The Bill camera crew to record.

basis throughout the year. At all times there are three separate colour-coded film units – red, blue and green – working simultaneously, each with its own producer and director, plus a team of script editors who work closely with the sixty-odd freelance writers who pen the episodes. The three colour-coded units flag up their territory on the set by using triangular signs carefully positioned around the cavernous offices. Their use is vital in order to ensure that the carefully sculpted order of the busy workplace is clear to all at a glance. Three individual hour-long episodes of The Bill are being filmed at the same time over every two-week period, and everyone must know which team they are with and which episode they are working on. The scale of the operation is massive: from my own experience of TV drama it appears to be ten times bigger than any other production.

'It's a very complex operation,' acknowledges executive producer Richard Handford, 'but everyone has learned by experience. Each time the series expands you know intuitively what you need to do to make it work. But I don't think that outside this building people are aware of how complex an operation it actually is.

'I know the colour coding sounds terribly primary schoolish,' he continues, 'but actually it really works because it means the walk-ons get on the right bus to the location, and the producers know which bits of paper are relevant to them and which are not.'

Handford, formerly an executive producer on Peak Practice, took over the reins at The Bill from long-standing executive producer Michael Chapman in November 1997. 'Michael was inspirational,' Handford says. 'I had worked for him as one of the

Left: **PC Harker investigates a disturbance in an episode entitled 'Weekends are for Wimps'.**
Below left: **Undercover desperado DC Rod Skase, played by Iain Fletcher, investigates a smuggling operation.**
Below: **Sgt Cryer has had to deal with many a tricky situation in his day. In 1985 he was taken hostage by a volatile gunman.**

facilitate, because a lot of the new ideas were already in the ether.'

But it was some months after his installation before The Bill was ready to launch its new one-hour format in summer 1998, and introduce new casting and story ideas. 'We had a nine-month gestation period,' explains Handford. 'It took that long to turn the proverbial oil tanker around just because the machine was so big and there were so many scripts and ideas in the pipeline.'

This new era includes new members of the cast like female detective Kerry Holmes and her witty and wily colleague Duncan Lennox, plus the return of old favourites like the rogue DCI Frank Burnside, who is as mean, tough and irresistible as ever.

Burnside achieved Bill immortality by shoving suspects' heads down toilets and firing choice insults at them, such as 'You slag!' Actor Chris Ellison feels that the public would have been disappointed to find that Burnside had mellowed during his time away from the

producers, and he had very clear views of what he wanted and what he thought the programme was and was not good at.'

On taking up his new position, Handford nevertheless felt that it was time for The Bill to move on. 'What I did was to ease certain constraints, and to

In an episode called 'Target Man', PC Hollis is quick to score when he gets the cuffs on villain Miller.

Top: **The Bill's first ever episode is 1983's 'Woodentop'. Trudie Goodwin makes her debut as PC June Ackland and Mark Wingett first appears as PC Jim Carver.**
Bottom: **Sgt Boyden and PC Page have a tough time negotiating their way out of a hostage crisis in the station.**

show over the past few years 'undercover in Manchester'. 'I believe his time up north means that he has even more to hide. Manchester was very tough, especially as he was literally living with villains all the time. There would have been plenty of sticky situations so he'll probably return even harder than before – if that's possible.'

Ellison has enjoyed being reunited with old friends and colleagues like Mark Wingett, who has played Jim Carver since The Bill's pilot episode 'Woodentop', broadcast in 1983. Still very much a key character, in an episode shown in May 1999 called 'Back To Basics', DC Carver faces the difficult career issue of 'tenure', which is a chance for CID officials to pull their detectives back into line by returning them to the streets. 'It is,' explains Richard Handford, 'effectively a way of making sure that CID people do

DC Jim Carver in an undercover drugs operation in Manchester, just before his transfer back into uniform which marks the beginning of a personal crisis.
Left: **DS Boulton, played by Russell Boulter, in an episode in which he partners dodgy detective Don Beech in a bid to put away a dealer in stolen goods.**

not get too big for their boots.'

This crisis for Carver is a good opportunity for the programme makers to revisit the DC's character and see where he is going. 'Actually,' confides Handford, 'in the real police this type of move is seen, as in our story, as a bit of a demotion, so Carver is going to have a hard time and sink to the depths before clawing back in due course. But he will not redeem himself for some

time and people will be speculating as to what happens to him.'

One of The Bill's great strengths is its strong ensemble cast, unsullied by difficult 'stars'. Actor Russell Boulter (DS Boulton) is impressed with the programme's commitment to realism and truthfulness in drama, and believes that the strengths of the writers and directors make it truly unbeatable. Add to this the fact that the show is pre-watershed and it is recognised that The Bill is a programme an entire family can sit down and watch together. 'There's something in it for the mums,' says Boulter, 'something for the dads and something for the children.'

THE USUAL SUSPECTS

Trudie Goodwin
SGT JUNE ACKLAND

Scott Neal
PC LUKE ASHTON

Billy Murray
DS DON BEECH

Russell Boulter
DS JOHN BOULTON

Tony O'Callagan
SGT MATTHEW BOYDON

Peter Ellis
CH. SUPERINTENDENT CHARLES BROWNLOW

Shaun Scott
DI CHRIS DEAKIN

Caroline Catz
DS ROSIE FOX

Huw Higginson
PC GEORGE GARFIELD

Karl Collins plays
DC DANNY GLAZE

Samantha Robson
PC VICKY HAGEN

Matthew Crompton
PC SAM HARKER

Colin Tarrant
INSPECTOR ANDREW MONROE

Lisa Geoghan
PC POLLY PAGE

Gregory Donaldson
DC TOM PROCTOR

Andrew Paul
PC DAVE QUINNAN

Libby Davison
DC LIZ RAWTON

Suzanne Maddock
PC CASS RICKMAN

Christopher Ellison
DCI FRANK BURNSIDE

Mark Wingett
DC JIM CARVER

Ben Roberts
CH. INSPECTOR
DEREK CONWAY

Eric Richard
SGT BOB CRYER

Ray Ashcroft
DS GEOFF DALY

Jeff Stewart
PC REG HOLLIS

Joy Brook
DC KERRY HOLMES

George Rossi
DC DUNCAN LENNOX

Clive Wedderburn
PC GARY McCANN

Simon Rouse
DCI JACK MEADOWS

Michael Higgs
PC EDDIE SANTINI

Iain Fletcher
DC ROD SKASE

Alex Walkinshaw
PC DALE SMITH

Graham Cole
PC TONY STAMP

Jane Wall
PC DI WORRELL

In 'Pond Life', The Bill investigates the effect of a recently released child molester on the local community. PCs Santini, Stamp and Garfield hold back the crowd.

'Our previous executive producer, Michael Chapman, saw it like a ship,' explains production manager Derek

Cotty. 'He treated us like a crew – roughly and hard, with a dedicated drop of

rum when the time was due – and it has worked very well ever since.'

There are four weeks of preparation before an episode is ready to be filmed. During these crucial weeks the production crew gradually come together, the script is finalised, budgets are agreed, locations are selected and 'recce'd'. Then, the guest characters in the script are cast and production and budgeting meetings are held. All this activity is finally resolved at a meeting before the start of the shoot which is attended by everybody involved, including the regular cast.

'Making a television programme or a film is very much like baking a cake,' confides production manager Derek Cotty, who has been a key member of The Bill team for sixteen years, from the very beginning of the show. 'You can get a book, you can get all the ingredients and put them all in and do what it says, but sometimes it rises and sometimes it doesn't. That's to do with the expertise of the chef. We have such a good team of people here, under a very good executive producer, that nine times out of ten the cake rises. It's all down to the planning and organisation.'

For Richard Handford, there are two main challenges to face in order to keep The Bill afloat. The first is to provide the impressive volume of high-standard material required by the network – feeding the machine. 'It's a very greedy monster. We need so many scripts to keep us going, it is an enormous task.'

As with any drama series there is a certain script failure rate. At The Bill, Handford must commission between eighty and ninety scripts per year to maintain an annual output of over seventy episodes. 'There is not more than a ten per cent failure rate, as we try to work with the writers and straighten them out. But it is a monstrous quantity.'

The Bill has always enjoyed a reputation in the business for the quality of its scripts. 'The quality drops at our peril. The greatest challenge is to say, "No, this isn't good, this isn't right yet so we won't do it." But, if you're going to say that, you have to have another script you can do just to keep the machine rolling on.'

Handford's other objective is somehow to schedule the production process so that the three colour-coded units can all operate simultaneously, despite needing to use the same actors and the same sets. Most dramas are made one at a time and

New member of the Sun Hill squad: executive producer Richard Handford with actors Graham Cole, Billy Murray and Scott Neal.

follow a linear pattern, each individual episode finished before the next is started. In comparison, the way The Bill operates – constantly juggling artists and location to satisfy demand – makes it more like a soap opera. 'If you've got three units all shooting at the same time, all three units want to occupy the custody area, or want to work with Sergeant Cryer at the same time, it's a very complex problem to sort out,' explains Handford.

It is the crucial job of project co-ordinator Nigel Wilson to work out the schedule for each unit and actor so that episodes can be filmed efficiently and on time. Wilson's office resembles what you might imagine the inside of a computer terminal to look like – a maze of coloured cards pasted on charts that spread right the way around the four walls of a fair-sized room. Nigel himself is a wealth of information. Ask him about an episode in which there is an explosion in a night club and in which there are at least three regular characters, and he moves without hesitation to a large board to the left. Pointing to a column of coloured cards, he declares, 'That's the green unit, a night shoot on Thursday week.'

The job involves going through each script and working out mathematically how he can get each actor from unit to unit and location to location. 'We cannot use a computer,' sighs Wilson. 'If it broke down it would be a disaster!'

A small but well-stocked bar is prominent to the side of his desk. 'That's for when something goes wrong and my brilliant plans have to go out of the window,' he concedes. 'Like the time when Mark Wingett's girlfriend gave birth a week early and it was Armageddon.'

There are three producers working at any one time, each responsible for a one-hour episode of The Bill every fortnight. Each producer works with

DC Carver at his best, dealing with an assault.

a production manager who is responsible for the day-to-day management of the sizable film unit working on location, as the producer is mainly tied up with the scripts. 'Our previous executive producer, Michael Chapman, saw it like a ship,' explains Derek Cotty. 'He treated us like a crew – roughly and hard, with a dedicated drop of rum when the time was due – and it has worked very well ever since.'

Richard Handford oversees the producers, and is drawn into the production process if further suggestions are needed or if there are any problems and somebody needs to make a unilateral decision. But Handford insists that it is a team effort rather than a vertical hierarchy. 'When it comes to casting new regular characters I work with the producers. If we wish to develop new storylines then it's a mixture of Julie Dixon and Alex Perrin in the script department, representing the script side, the producers and myself. Julie and Alex pool all the ideas from all the script editors and together we decide what we will and won't do.'

The Bill does not cover stories that cannot be

Extreme violence is treated with subtlety, to permit pre-watershed transmission, but to maximum effect.

put out in the pre-watershed, eight o'clock slot. So if an idea is put forward that requires extreme violence, or sexual contact, or very strong language then, though it is rare, the team have to reject the project. However, Handford and his team do try to find ways of dealing with good ideas in a fashion acceptable to The Bill. 'We don't have to confront violence or sex head-on, we can allude to it without actually having to show it.'

In the recent 'Badlands' episode, for example, in which PC Quinnan is savagely beaten and stabbed by a gang of youths, the programme managed to tackle extreme violence without actually showing a great deal. Much of the violence was implied – as an audience we knew the characters of the injured Quinnan and the frustrated PC Garfield in sufficient depth to *feel* their pain and frustration rather than need to be shown it.

With the new one-hour format the programme makers now have more scope to develop the personal lives of the regular characters. Richard Handford emphasises, however, that the longer episodes were re-introduced not only for reasons of character development, but as a forum for stronger, more challenging storylines. 'We were going to concentrate anyway on our characters and their professional lives and relationships, and not let our guest characters have all the best lines. The one-hours are co-incidental. The thinking behind the series had already changed – this was part of my plan to move the show on.'

To some extent the team has to choose which episode to make when on the basis of which actors are available when, but Handford does not favour the approach of simply swapping characters around. 'If you could just at a stroke change Garfield's name and make it Quinnan, and not change a word of dialogue, then we would just be writing for cardboard cut-outs. So I resist changes of this kind. If it's a story about Boyden having an affair with an underage girl, we can't possibly say, "Well, we'll have it with Cryer!" The idea is unthinkable.'

For veteran Bill scriptwriter Elizabeth-Anne Wheal the story is the most important consideration: an episode must work as a piece of drama before it can be thought of as a police story. Another pertinent factor is to make the episode fit into the territory in which The Bill is comfortable: 'We're not going to go out and spend money on lots of effects, we're not going to do big crime stories. It's going to be small day-to-day crimes that happen next door to everyone, and it's about doing something with that.'

Following in the tradition of all the best English police shows from Z Cars onwards, Wheal likes to deal 'in a fly on the wall way, with ordinary stories about ordinary people and coppers, and what happens'.

A middle-class, university-educated, rather forthright ex-hippie, Wheal found that she had a very negative attitude to the police before she started writing for The Bill. 'It changed a lot once I started meeting police officers,' she confesses. 'Nowadays, I've found that it is tremendously interesting getting inside the Metropolitan Police. It has surprised me hugely in terms of characters and situations.'

Wheal does all her own story research, spending memorable days out and about with the Brixton police. 'I had two days out in area cars, and two days with the CID, including a hair-raising incident in a warehouse where an armed man was running around. They make you sign a form – something like, If you get shot it's not our fault! It is scary.'

As a writer she feels that if you walk into any kind of 'world' there will be a lot of fascinating human stories. 'In the police it is the same, though it has opened my eyes and made me think about a lot of the more serious issues involving policing and law and order. There is a massive world there to play with and, in a way, you can choose to play with any aspect of it you like. The policing does not have to be directly relevant – as in my recent stories on the theme of sexual harassment at work. I write about

PC Stamp is faced with a crisis when he reverses his area car at speed over a pedestrian. The accident is pulled off with the use of a stunt man and a dummy to take the impact of the car.

the police a lot, but actually what I am doing is writing about one of any number of things that interests or concerns me at the time.'

What most interests Wheal is all the grey areas, not only in terms of corruption, but in terms of life experience for policemen. 'Where does one's own personal sense of what is right and what is wrong come into conflict with what one's been taught or trained to do?' she asks, and, 'What

happens if you're a by-the-book copper who gets tricked?'

Wheal thinks that today policing is one of the toughest jobs anyone could be asked to do, because society's expectations of police officers are so high. 'They are the front-line response service for what used to be a very simple question of keeping the villains locked up, and is now a very complex set of

problems about our society.' The police, she feels, are now grappling with issues to do with how we view people in society in terms of class, race and mental health. 'They are the first line of response in a society that is essentially going through a crisis. The Stephen Lawrence case absolutely reflects that.'

Wheal is best known for her ability to tell a rip-roaring tale. Her Fox/Santini storyline, on the theme of a sexual harassment and assault in the workplace, started off the 1998 new autumn season of one-hour episodes and was a tremendous success. 'It was a bit like picking up a great big carrier and steaming it off in a different direction, with the scheduling and the work that had to be done in the production office.'

Writing the three one-hour follow-up episodes for summer 1999 has been a great chance for her to come back and work with characters and situations she has already spent time with. On a drama series of this multi-episodic nature it is quite unusual and challenging to be able to tell three hours of continuous television drama: 'Particularly in the environment of The Bill which is one of the best if

Top: **Richard Handford has brought in many new, dynamic characters to liven up Sun Hill. Popular new recruit PC Vicky Hagen behind the scenes with a make-up artist.**
Bottom: **An anxious PC Stamp is cleared of causing death by dangerous driving, but faces internal disciplinary proceedings. It could be the end of his career.**

not *the* best writing outlet in terms of professionalism and everyone working in the same direction.'

For Richard Handford, ultimately satisfaction lies in developing a highly entertaining episode. 'We are in the business to entertain,' he says, 'which doesn't mean we are here to make people laugh. People are entertained by even the darkest, bleakest stories. Our greatest satisfaction is to know we've entertained the viewers and that they are saying, "That was a cracking episode, I've really enjoyed it!"'

Top left: **Elizabeth-Anne Wheal's major story of sexual assault. In an episode entitled 'Deep End', smouldering PC Santini becomes increasingly obsessed with PC Rosie Fox.**
Top: **A post-Christmas lull turns into a chaotic shift for PCs Vicky Hagen and Dave Quinnan.**
Above: **Burnside is back, to popular acclaim – a ladies' man trying to pin down high-class hookers in 'Betrayal'.**

Police Lingo

A BODY	An arrest ('I've nicked a body')
ALCO	Anything to do with the breath test procedure
AMIP	Area Major Incident Pool
APPO	Area Press and Publicity Officer
ARB	Accident Report Book
ARV	Armed Response Unit
THE BIG HOUSE	Crown Court
BLACK RAT	Traffic Patrol Officer
BLAGGER	Robber
BLO	Borough Liaison Officer
BRAINS DEPT	CID (as referred to by Uniform)
BUTTON MOB	Uniform Officer (as referred to by CID)
CAD	Computer Aided Despatch
CID	Criminal Investigation Department
CIVVIES	Civilian support staff
CRIS	Crime Reporting Information System (replaced crime sheets)
CSG	Crime Support Group
CORRES	Correspondence/paperwork
DIPPERS	Pickpockets
DRUM	House
DSE	Divisional Scene Examiner
ESSO	Every Saturday and Sunday off
FACTORY	Police station
FATACC	Fatal Accident
FENCE	Person to whom stolen good are taken
FME	Forensic Medical Examiner
GOING UP THE ROAD	Refers to Crown Court
GP	General Purpose (used for unmarked vehicle)
HANDLING	Handling stolen goods
HAVE IT ON YOUR TOES or DANCERS	Run away
HORTI	A request to produce driving documents derived from form HORT1 aka Producer
IC 1– 6	Identity Codes (nationality)
T CALL	An urgent call to police that is graded as Immediate response

IR	Information Room
IRB	Incident Report Book (also used for arrests)
MISPER	Missing Person
M2MP	Full Call Sign for Main Set Channel for Information Room
MSS	Message Switching System
NCPA	No cause for Police Action
NDIU	National Drugs Intelligence Unit
NFA	No Further Action
NIB	National Identification Bureau
NON DESCRIPT	Observation vehicle (or 'Nondy')
NSY	New Scotland Yard
OB	Occurrence Book
OBBO	Observation
OP	Observation Point
OPPO	Mate (someone you're paired with for specialist tasks)
OSCAR	Call Sign for Traffic Control on Main Set
OTS	Over The Side (seeing someone for a bit of hanky panky!)
PACE	Police And Criminal Evidence Act
PARS	Particulars of an occurrence
PIMP or PONCE	Someone living off earnings from prostitution
PLONKS	Women police officers
PNC	Police National Computer
POLACC	Police Accident
PRs	Personal Radios
PROCESS	Anything to do with reporting motorists
REFS	Canteen breaks
RUN IN	Yard where stolen goods/vehicles are housed
S CALL	A call to police that is graded as Soon response
SARGE or SKIP	Sergeant (NOT 'Skipper')
SPIN	Search
TI	Trainee Investigator
TSG	Territorial Support Group
W	Warrant
WHEELS	Motor vehicle
WOODENTOPS	Uniform Officers (as referred to by CID)
	NB: 'Woodentop' was also the title of the pilot episode of The Bill
YACS	Youth and Community Section
THE YARD	New Scotland Yard

The Sun Hill squad in pantomime costume for the 1997 production of *Widow Twanky*.

A wealth of actors have played their part in making The Bill the enormous success it is. With a cast of thirty regulars and more than a thousand juicy roles a year for guest actors to play, for actors the programme has become something of a national institution. Even stars like Rik Mayall, Ronald Pickup, Lorraine Chase and Glynis Barber have been happy to take on the role of a villain on The Bill. 'In fact,' confides casting director Lisa Harris, 'it is a running joke at Bosun House that if you look at the

actors' biographies in any West End theatre programme, they will all have included a stint on The Bill.'

'THE RELIEF'
UNIFORM PCs

SCOTT NEAL plays

PC LUKE ASHTON

'I like PC Ashton,' says baby-faced lad-about-town Scott Neal, 'because he's so different from everyone else. He's very innocent and he tries very hard, but he still messes up.'

Though a much liked member of the squad, Ashton is wet behind the ears and learning the hard way. In an early episode, 'Humpty Dumpty', he tries in vain to tempt a character played by Rik Mayall down from a roof, and feels devastated when he fails. More recently, in another episode entitled 'Kiss Chase', a witness accuses him of getting her pregnant and he is forced to admit to his senior officers that he has slept with her, even though he is not the child's father.

At a mere twenty-one years old, Scott Neal has already been in the business for ten years. He trained at the Anna Scher Theatre School, where he was in the same class as EastEnders star Patsy Palmer. During that time he played a plethora of small TV roles in shows like EastEnders and Bramwell. His first major role was alongside London Bridge actor Glen Berry in the film *Beautiful Thing*, in which two teenage boys fall in love. 'A lot of guys tried it on with me after the film,' Neal admits with a grin. 'They chat you up or flirt with you, but I just have to laugh with it. They think they know me, but it is the character they are in love with.'

Last year Neal spent two months in India filming the as yet to be released film *Wonderland*. This helped inspire a love of travel and he has since been to Bali, Australia and the Seychelles. 'I try to go to a different place each time, to really explore the world.'

In flying the nest, he is leaving both Mum in Islington and The Bill to try his luck in America. 'I've learnt so much here, and the people have been fantastic,' he enthuses, 'but I want to move on and learn something else. It will be a whole new beginning.'

PC Ashton, after failing to prevent an ex-crack addict kill his daughter and himself, leaves the Police force, having decided he isn't cut out for it.

HUW HIGGINSON plays

PC GEORGE GARFIELD

PC George Garfield is a steady, reliable type, known for his loyalty and integrity. 'He takes pride in his work,' actor Huw Higginson elaborates. 'His best quality is his commitment to his colleagues. He doesn't let anybody down. Garfield acts as a trouble shooter for the team.'

But Garfield can also be something of a bull in a china shop, charging in wildly before he has properly thought through the repercussions of his actions. 'There is a lot of humour attached to those aspects of his character, and I enjoy that.'

Thirty-five-year-old Welsh-born Higginson, who comes from a theatrical family, has played the part of Garfield for ten years and leaves the series in 1999 to pursue other projects. Recently Garfield has enjoyed several romantic attachments with women: a two-part story in which he becomes involved with a female newspaper reporter, and a romantic triangle with Quinnan and the nurse who brought him back to health following his stabbing, with whom they are both in love. Garfield departs Sun Hill in the wake of that failed romance.

'I live in a house full of women – which is interesting!' declares Higginson of his own home life with a grin. He is a great deal more successful romantically than Garfield, and lives with his wife Geraldine who prefers to be known as 'Gel', a former stage manager at The Bill, and their children. 'We've got two girls, Meg, who is four and my stepdaughter Sarah, who is thirteen.'

When he is not rushing around on a Saturday morning getting 'the girls' breakfast in bed, he seeks out male company usually in the shape of his father, former RSC actor Tim Wilton, and they head off to see the rugby match at his local Twickenham ground. Otherwise, his great passion is football. 'I'm a Season Ticket holder at Chelsea, so Andy Paul and I have fascinating mornings talking football non-stop.'

However, their friendship nearly came to an abrupt halt when Paul took him to a recent Arsenal versus Chelsea game. 'We beat them five-nil at their ground,' crows Higginson. 'It's the first time that has happened in about seventy years!'

SAMANTHA ROBSON plays

PC VICKY HAGEN

PC Vicky Hagen came to Sun Hill just over a year ago from an Essex nick, where she had seen all her service to date. A qualified area car driver, Hagen is subject to a lot of prejudice from the male officers, as very few women are allowed to do the course. Samantha Robson, who plays PC Hagen, explains that Hagen's punchy tenacity, combined with the action of being a driver, is what makes being in The Bill so great. 'I do all my own stunts, having done the Advanced Precision Driving course at Hendon. And I get to play at being a policewoman, which is what I wanted to be as a teenager but did not have the courage to do. I get to be the type of woman I would kill to be. It's very exciting.'

Like Hagen, Robson is something of an action woman, enjoying sports such as scuba diving and mountain biking. She runs every day and cycles to and fro between her south-London home and work.

Robson was brought up in south London on a Wandsworth housing estate by a single mother, and has two older brothers who provided a strong male influence. Determined to succeed, she trained at the Guilford School of Acting, followed by a two-year stint with the Royal Shakespeare Company.

When Robson joined The Bill her character was described as very tough and straightforward: 'She was the kind of woman who was my equal,' Robson enthused, 'but the character has progressed, and she has become very bitchy towards other women. She definitely has a problem with them, not because she feels threatened, but because she wants other women to behave as she does. She makes strong judgements on other women.' However, Hagen's character takes a different turn when she becomes involved with PC Santini, and we see this rather masculine policewoman become soft and vulnerable.

Robson, at twenty-seven, has a successful, long-term relationship with an actor, whose name she will not divulge. She plans to stay with the show as long as she's enjoying it and still learning from it. 'Eventually I do want to have a career and a home and a child if it's possible.'

MATTHEW CROMPTON plays

PC SAM HARKER

Matthew Crompton, who joined The Bill in 1998, is much like the Liverpool-born character of Sam Harker whom he plays. Both are easy-going, laid-back and friendly, and both come from large close families. It seems perfect casting for the twenty-something actor who lives in a north-west London flatshare and likes nothing better than to relax with a can of beer and his bass guitar.

PC Harker always knew what he would do with his life, coming from a long line of policemen – back in Liverpool, his father is a copper and so is his elder brother. As far as he is concerned, it beats working for a living! With a ready smile, it is clear that he relishes the job. Having spent five years with the rather specialist Heathrow police, he transferred to Sun Hill to broaden his experience with a spell at an East End station. Single, with a naturally friendly manner, he is not easily fazed by any situation.

Members of the public find PC Harker thoughtful and straightforward in his dealings with them, and locally he has rapidly become a popular and respected uniformed beat bobby. He also has the sense to leave the troubles of policing at work with his uniform at the end of the shift, and finds it easy to relax with his mates and a beer.

Like Harker, Crompton is happy at work. 'I love being in The Bill,' he enthuses. 'It was brilliant landing such a good part and I love wearing the uniform – it gives me loads of confidence. But when I get home I just like a laugh with my mates.' Recently he split up amicably with his girlfriend of six years, Jan, because he did not feel ready to settle down. Now he mainly likes to go out with his friends and have a good time, clubbing, drinking and having a good time. 'My ideal girl is one with a pulse,' he jokes, though he admits he would like a girl who can make him laugh.

Before The Bill, Crompton worked extensively in the theatre, then became a children's presenter on Saturday Disney. He went on to become a household name as Darren Murphy, Jacqui Dixon's drug-addict boyfriend in the Merseyside soap Brookside. But gaining a part in the long-running police series he had watched as a child still made him quake. 'I was shaking like a leaf in my first scene. I was just glad that I wasn't doing a canteen scene with a cup of coffee in my hand, as it would have gone all over me.'

JEFF STEWART plays

PC REG HOLLIS

Bachelor Jeff Stewart, in his early forties, has played The Bill's bumbling PC Hollis for the best part of fourteen years. He won his earliest acting award while still at primary school – for impersonating a fish.

Stewart continues to enjoy the role. One of the better moments he recalls happened when a stray fan in an old mac sidled up to him in Sloane Square, near his Chelsea home, and said out of the side of his mouth, 'Ollis, if you was my collator, I'd 'ave you shot.'

'Obviously an off-duty policeman,' concluded Stewart, unable to keep a straight face.

Born in Aberdeen Jeff Stewart originally went to college to study History of Art before finding his vocation at London's Drama Centre. Dropping out early on in the course, when he found himself falling asleep in lectures, he decided that a more practical approach to acting would be right for him and soon landed a job at the Cambridge Theatre as an assistant stage manager. It was not long before he was acting in television shows like Crossroads, Minder, Give Us a Break, Dr Who, and his all time favourite, Hi de Hi.

PC Reg Hollis is one of life's persistent moaners. He enjoys the gossip round the station and is always ready to initiate alarm and despondency even when there is no need for it. This tendency doesn't make him a popular figure amongst the squad, although there is overall a strange fondness for his lack of guile.

Hollis was at one time the station's 'Federation' man – Sun Hill's representative to the Police Federation – initially because no one else wanted the job. But he, naturally, took the job very seriously and at times proved to be very useful in the role. It is perhaps for this reason that he retains some loyal friends amongst his colleagues, despite his moaning. Recently, in the face of a distinct lack of interest from colleagues – only old stalwarts like Brownlow try to encourage him – Hollis has been setting up a Sun Hill website. The rest of his colleagues are hard pushed to take him seriously.

Inevitably Reg Hollis is a hypochondriac, suffering variously from headache, backache, neckache and even the odd stomach-ache, which he likes to blame on the station canteen. His eccentric hobbies include miniature railways and tending the Sun Hill garden.

For actor Jeff Stewart, the part is a gift. 'Hollis is funny without even knowing it. He's enthusiastic, but his enthusiasm bubbles up in some funny places.' Burnside once remarked of him, when he seemed inordinately pleased to have discovered the remains of what might have been a mass murder burial site: 'There's definitely something unhealthy about you, Hollis.'

Stewart is stunned by the number of women who really like Hollis. 'I have even had a number of marriage proposals but naturally I don't do anything about them. After all, the girls don't know the real me. They are in love with Reg.'

CLIVE WEDDERBURN plays

PC GARY McCANN

Thirty-year-old PC Gary McCann joined the police force as a graduate, having gained a degree in Politics and History from the University of East Anglia. However, he soon rejected academia in favour of a police career, keen to see action rather than indulge in theory.

Birmingham-born actor Clive Wedderburn trained at the East 15 Acting School. After a bit of local theatre and appearing in TV dramas he was snapped up to play PC McCann at The Bill. McCann is portrayed as clever, but without arrogance, and Wedderburn has tried to invest him with his own father's strength of character. Wedderburn senior, a taxi-driver, at one time worked at a crisis centre. 'One night, when I was a kid,' explains Wedderburn, 'some guy reeking of meths tried to take a swing at him. It frightened me to death and I ran away to hide. But my dad didn't show any fear. He knew he didn't have to meet violence with violence. He just calmed the man down with common sense.'

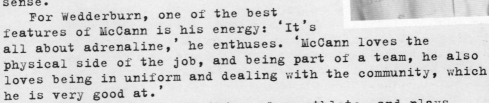

For Wedderburn, one of the best features of McCann is his energy: 'It's all about adrenaline,' he enthuses. 'McCann loves the physical side of the job, and being part of a team, he also loves being in uniform and dealing with the community, which he is very good at.'

The actor is also something of an athlete, and plays football regularly, both for his local side and for The Bill. The Bill team can often be found playing charity matches on any Saturday when enough of the actors can manage to squeeze a day off! Wedderburn is also known fondly by his colleagues as 'the mounted policeman', due to his passion for riding in London's Hyde Park – not because of the park's upper-crust connotations, Wedderburn hastens to add, but because it has the most convenient stables to his north of the river flat-share.

LISA GEOGHAN plays

PC POLLY PAGE

Sun Hill's chirpy blonde cockney policewoman, the kind but tough PC Polly Page, is played by Bermondsey-based actress Lisa Geoghan. 'Polly is much tougher than me,' says Geoghan. 'She's not scared of anything, whereas I would run a mile if I encountered any trouble whatsoever. I'd also find myself taking every sad case home with me!'

Bill writers say of Page that she is 'Gutsy, sharp, with a keen South London humour, Page has few illusions about the job and is eager for experience in all its aspects.'

'Page joined the police because she believes she can make a difference, even if it means being punched in the face,' explains Geoghan. The policewoman's dedication is unswerving. A Londoner through and through she has set her sights on tackling the low-life of the metropolis, and not on migrating to more parochial climes.

PC Page's life revolves completely around her job, which she sees as far more important than any boyfriend. 'My only regret for her is that she never has any decent men in her life and there is no sign of a lasting romance coming her way,' confides Geoghan. Page's last failed romance, in a 1998 three-parter called 'Tainted Love', was with someone who turned out to be a conman. Geoghan, in contrast, has lived with her postman husband Michael Power for thirteen years, having first met him when they were at primary school together. Although the couple have very different careers, she insists her husband's colleagues do not think of her job as special. 'Michael doesn't take much notice of what I do,' she smiles. 'He gets a bit of stick from his mates, but only as much stick as he gives them about their girlfriends!'

Though content with her husband and home life, Geoghan defines herself primarily as an actress. At thirty-two she is in no hurry to have children, admitting, 'There is so much going on at the moment, we haven't got round to it yet, but I'm sure we will have kids one day. My brother's children have got me thinking about it.

Working on The Bill has made her more aware of the problems the police face in terms of dealing with difficult children in the community. In cases such as child drug abuse she takes a tough line, believing that parents should take more responsibility. 'The police are unfairly criticised for not doing their job properly. But parents need to be more clued up and shouldn't assume their kids are angels.'

ANDREW PAUL plays

PC DAVE QUINNAN

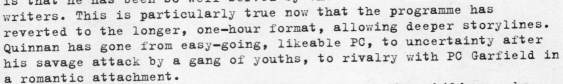

The unassuming Andy Paul started acting when he
was fourteen, with a small part in a TV
adaptation of a Graham Greene story produced by
Thames in 1975. Before that, he attended the
famous Anna Scher Children's Theatre School in
London's East End, breeding ground of so many
EastEnders and Grange Hill stars. He feels that
the best thing about playing Quinnan, which he
has been doing for ten years – 'man and boy' –
is that he has been so well served by the
writers. This is particularly true now that the programme has
reverted to the longer, one-hour format, allowing deeper storylines.
Quinnan has gone from easy-going, likeable PC, to uncertainty after
his savage attack by a gang of youths, to rivalry with PC Garfield in
a romantic attachment.

PC Dave Quinnan is a south Londoner, one of five children, who
joined the force in 1986 after originally training as an electrician.
Money was the chief reason he changed profession; he was attracted by
the substantial pay increases granted the police service under the
Thatcher government. But Quinnan is a generous man, always ready to
help his mother and always first at the bar to buy a round of drinks.
For Quinnan, police work is about keeping the peace and punishing
wrongdoers. He's not an
idealist, but he enjoys wearing
the uniform and the authority it
gives him. More than anything,
Quinnan is charming and good at
sizing people up and giving them
what they want. He is also a
single man who is attractive
and knows it.

Paul, on the other hand, has
been with his wife Laura for
twenty years, and they have
three boys, Ben, Freddie and
Joe. An avid Arsenal supporter,
he has two Season Tickets and
takes the boys in turns to
matches. He sees himself as a
normal husband and father.
'I'm an actor because it was
something I was good at at school and something I always wanted to
do. It's a job, one that I'm fortunate enough to enjoy. I'm not very
glamorous, I just like going home at the end of the day.'

SUZANNE MADDOCK plays

PC CASS RICKMAN

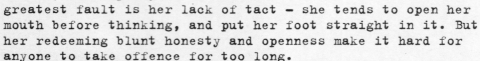

At twenty-two, PC Cass Rickman, who grew up amongst a large family in a chaotic Liverpool terrace, has already been in the force for four years. Transferring to the Met has given Rickman her first chance to live away from home and she arrives at Sun Hill full of such tremendous energy and enthusiasm that some of the older stalwarts of the squad find it both exhausting and irritating. However, with her quick wit and lively nature, she rapidly makes friends. Her greatest fault is her lack of tact – she tends to open her mouth before thinking, and put her foot straight in it. But her redeeming blunt honesty and openness make it hard for anyone to take offence for too long.

For young Liverpudlian actress Suzanne Maddock, who has recently been seen in episodes of Casualty and Hetty Wainthrop Investigates, winning the part of PC Rickman has been a dream come true. 'I couldn't believe it when they told me I had got the part,' she raves. 'I have watched The Bill since I was a little girl and next minute I'm acting with them all! They are all fantastic actors and have made me really welcome.'

For Maddox, like her alter-ego Rickman, the part involved a move south. 'I moved down from the Wirral especially for this role and it is the first time I have moved away from home. My character is fun and I think her feisty nature will lead to some great storylines.'

Rickman left school early clutching only a handful of GCSEs, a bright but easily distracted teenager who spent too much time skiving and going out with the boys. When she grew bored with a dull job in an insurance company and got the sack following too many late nights and non-appearances in the mornings, her exasperated father persuaded her to apply to the police. But she failed the interview. This stopped her in her tracks and made her think – she had seen enough of the job by now to want it. Quickly, she re-applied and got in. Now PC Rickman loves her job and takes pride in doing it well. She has arrived at Sun Hill determined to make her mark, and with characteristic verve intends to enjoy herself too.

MICHAEL HIGGS plays

PC EDDIE SANTINI

Actor Michael Higgs describes his character, PC
Eddie Santini, as a bit of a rogue. 'In the
early episodes, a year ago, his Italian good
looks proved irresistible to female colleagues
– which at the time got up the noses of the
other policemen at the nick.' Now things have
changed, and he is viewed by all with a great
deal of suspicion.

Santini has a wicked sense of humour,
which at first made him a likeable part of the
squad. But increasingly his humour has become
quite cutting, causing resentment. It appears
that he is something of a bully. As soon as
he could, Santini moved out of ordinary policing and
joined the crime squad in a south London divisional nick, wanting to be
where the action was. But after several years in the squad, mixing with
the old-school CID who taught him the best tricks in the book, it is
clear that Santini is a rule breaker. He arrived at Sun Hill, having been
turned down for CID because his DI did not trust him.

All this can be quite stressful for thirty-one-year-old Birmingham-
born Michael Higgs and, since taking on the role of Santini, he has
discovered the perfect way to relax – yoga. 'Yoga is an amazing activity
– it makes you feel exhilarated but really centred and calm all at the
same time. Eddie Santini would certainly benefit from a session or two.'

Despite the yoga, Higgs is by his own admission indecisive and
nervous. 'I'm just so worried about commitment,' he says. 'Even when I
was offered the part in The Bill I wasn't sure if I should take it. But
then I'm always like that with jobs. If I have to commit myself to
anything lasting more than four months, I begin to worry.'

Santini's popularity on the squad continues to dwindle, and he shows a
particularly nasty side of his character when he tries to becomes
romantically involved with pretty new recruit PC Rosie Fox. Working
closely with her on an undercover operation he pushes her too far and
refuses to back off when told. Despite Santini's initial attempts at
apology, Fox wants nothing more to do with him. She is furious, and it is
downhill all the way for their relationship and for Santini's behaviour
in general. He begins to take malicious delight in tormenting her, making
strange phone calls and spreading lies. Through Santini's character, The
Bill looks at the very real problem of sexual harassment within the
police force.

Six months later, as Santini continues to bully his fellow officers –
both male and female – he has become a recognised problem within the Sun
Hill squad. At the time of writing it looks like his days are numbered,
and now that he is awaiting trial for murder the future looks grim.

GRAHAM COLE plays

PC TONY STAMP

'PC Stamp is the kind of bloke that I would like to turn up if I'd been burgled,' reveals actor Graham Cole. 'He actually looks as though he's going to go and do something about it.'

Cole did fifteen years in repertory theatre before landing the part of Stamp in The Bill. He was starring in *Jesus Christ Superstar* when he was spotted by a Bill editor who said he must write to Peter Cregeen, the then producer, as he thought he would be perfect for a policeman they were casting. 'How he knew I don't know, as I had a great big beard at the time,' laughs Cole. 'I looked more like Makarios – the notorious Greek Cypriot Archbishop – than a policeman!'

Cole started his career in 1974 as a holiday camp Red Coat, and has retained his love of comedy. He likes nothing better than to raise money for charity by standing in front of a live audience, improvising. 'Though I would like to be a real copper, I couldn't do it. I couldn't take the verbals,' he laughs good naturedly. 'I have a very wicked sense of humour.'

PC Stamp on the other hand enjoys life as a beat copper, and has no interest in climbing up the career ladder if it means taking him away from the 'front line'. He is a conscientious officer, sometimes excessively so. 'He likes being a beat bobby,' Cole emphasises. 'He's like a god in his little area car.' Another thing that Cole makes clear is that Stamp has chosen to be in uniform. 'The perception is that the plain clothed officers are superior to the uniformed ones. It simply is not true. I think the backbone of the force are the guys on the streets in uniform. They are the ones the public meet.'

Cole sees Stamp as someone you can trust, but does not flinch from portraying the effect that life on the streets dealing with rough criminals and tough confrontations has had on him. 'When he enters a situation where he faces a gang of youths he's got to watch himself, he's got to survive. Stamp has been beaten up about four time in the series. I've been shot, stabbed, had fridges thrown at me...'

Unlike the single forty-something Stamp, Cole is married to Cherry, whom he met when she was sixteen and on holiday with her parents at Butlins where Cole was a Red Coat. They now have two children, Matthew, fifteen and Laura, thirteen. Though Stamp has enjoyed many romances over the years, Cole was unenthusiastic when producers suggested marrying him off.

'It's great to play an opposite. You don't become an actor to play yourself. I know what it's like to be married and have two kids. I've no idea what it's like not to go home to that kind of responsibility. Thank God for the day job! When you can't see that line between fiction and reality I think it's a bit sad.'

JANE WALL plays

PC DI WORRELL

When I spoke to Nigerian-born Jane Wall she had only been at The Bill for four weeks, but was clearly thrilled to be there. 'So far it is fantastic. I'm still getting to know the cast. I keep calling everyone by their character names because I've been a fan for so long. It's been quite exciting meeting them all.'

Di Worrell's a people person. She loves a gossip and a laugh and settles easily into male banter, while still remaining very much one of the girls. Few can resist her impish humour and it's not unknown for her to stir up some gossip mischievously in order to make a shift pass more quickly. Though she can sometimes push things a bit too far, she's usually an easy favourite among the relief – the uniform police officers on duty. Wall sums up her character, who has been in the force for eight years, as 'a bit of a flirt who likes gossip, but is very capable and good at her job'. Di Worrell, she explains, is ambitious 'but not to progress through the ranks. She wants to be involved in the job.'

PC Worrell was born and brought up in Stratford, east London, close to Sun Hill. She did not want to bump into old school friends while out on the beat, so made sure her first posting took her to the other side of London. By transferring to Sun Hill, though not exactly home turf, she is sufficiently near to her old haunts to know her way around the area, and to encounter people she has known all her life. After eight years on the force, she now has the confidence to cope with this familiarity. Pretty and petite, she's often assumed by male colleagues to need protecting. But she is quick on her feet and, if cornered, is a great deal tougher than she looks.

Always having known that she would dance or act for a living, Jane Wall, twenty-seven, graduated from drama school six years ago and has since done a lot of work in television drama. She has appeared in such programmes as Dangerfield and A Touch of Frost for the BBC, and Bliss for Carlton. However, she considers the part of PC Worrell her first major break, as it allows her the pleasure of developing a character over time.

She sees one of the strengths of The Bill reflected in the quantity of actors it employs. 'It's a great showcase for actors,' she says. 'There are very few dramas on television that have so many actors in them every week, in addition to the regulars. I think that is one of the things that make it so interesting.'

UNIFORM SERGEANTS
AND SENIOR OFFICERS

TRUDIE GOODWIN plays

SGT JUNE ACKLAND

Actress Trudie Goodwin has played the perceptive and sympathetic Sgt Ackland from the very first pilot show, Woodentop, in which she took the young probationer Carver under her wing. Despite sixteen years of playing a policewoman she feels she could never be one in reality. 'It's about the last thing that it would cross my mind to be. I don't feel authority sits terribly easily on my shoulders. I was a teacher a long time ago and exercising authority was partly why I didn't like that. I'm also inclined to get too personally involved with individuals, which as a policeman you can't afford to do.'

Goodwin, from south London, first went on the stage at Greenwich Youth Theatre when she was thirteen. Not a confident child, she nevertheless found it was something she could do well. Her parents, however, encouraged her to get a 'proper career', and she spent a year teacher training before finding herself a niche in Theatre in Education, which involved visiting schools around the country and putting on plays with the children.

Later she broadened her experience in repertory theatre in Coventry, Exeter and Leicester. While appearing in a production of Joe Orton's *Loot* she met and fell in love with her husband, the actor and now sitcom writer Kit Jackson. They married in 1979 and have two daughters, Jessica and Eleanor.

Since then the couple have only acted together once, in an episode of The Bill in 1995 in which Kit played a particularly odious character. 'He was horrible,' grimaces Goodwin, 'a thoroughly unpleasant bloke. He also had this dreadful costume on. I could imagine people asking, "Urghh is she married to him?"'

Goodwin says she regularly gets recognised in the street. 'People say: "You're just the sort of policewoman I would want to help me."' But for the actress, The Bill is very much a job and she enjoys going home to her family each day.

By comparison, the unmarried Ackland is always deeply involved in her work. For some years her own life was restricted as she cared for her invalid father, who recently died; she never took the time to think what her own personal needs might be. As a result, there is an inner core of loneliness which she takes care to keep hidden. Ackland, however, does have a lot of charm and is liked and respected by the lads of Sun Hill more than she realises.

'As an actress, to have a stable job with money coming in and to be doing what you want is great,' says Goodwin. She hopes that Ackland shows up a good side to the police, but adds: 'The worst thing is people confusing me with a real policewoman. The only similarity that exists between June and I is that we both give 110 per cent to our work.'

TONY O'CALLAGHAN plays

SGT MATTHEW BOYDEN

Forty-two-year-old Tony O'Callaghan smiles
when asked to comment on the character he
has been playing for the last seven years.
'He's opportunistic, a bit mischievous, a
bit obvious. He's good fun to play. He can
be relatively sensitive, has a heart. He's
also got a nasty side. If he is in trouble –
a panic situation and on a sinking ship – he
will tend to bring everyone down with him.'
However, Boyden's relaxed, easy-going
manner make him popular with his
colleagues, and a trusted member of the
team.

O'Callaghan lives with his wife Siobhan in north London, but
Boyden is fairly well known for his roving eye. An affair with a
probationer while at his sergeant's course in Hendon effectively
ended his marriage and made any rapid future promotion unlikely. He
no longer sees his daughter, and his wife has re-married. Later,
having eventually reached the rank of sergeant, another indiscretion
with a female DS forced his move from Romford to Sun Hill.

In the recent episode 'No Love Lost', while at a club, Boyden
boasts to PCs Ashton and Santini that he can get any girl there. This
leads to disaster when he takes a beautiful girl home with him, only
for it to transpire that she is just fifteen. To make matters worse,
the girl, from a criminal background, later kills herself.

O'Callaghan admits that he was nervous when he first read the
script. 'Then I thought, what a
brilliant storyline. It's probably
the best I've ever had. After all
those years of "Step this way" and
"Shut up", it's a gift.'

As far as O'Callaghan is
concerned, Boyden is a man who has
been hurt by past relationships and,
as a result, cannot commit. 'All that
bragging and chasing is just bravado.
We see his flat for the first time in
that episode – it's sad there's no
one to share it with him. And there
was a lot of remorse at the end of
the story which dragged him out of
the mire.' Boyden's regret helps the
audience empathise with his predicament, and we are left with the
sense that Boyden remains a decent and honest policeman.

PETER ELLIS plays

CH. SUPERINTENDENT CHARLES BROWNLOW

'It's odd playing the only character in The Bill that really has got no one else to relate to,' reflects the quietly spoken and – bearing in mind the stern, conventional figure he cuts on screen – surprisingly nice Peter Ellis.

As Ellis points out, Brownlow is an isolated character, originally conceived as a 'limited, conventional, unimaginative man, unquestioningly sympathetic to whatever directive the Commissioner's office issues'.

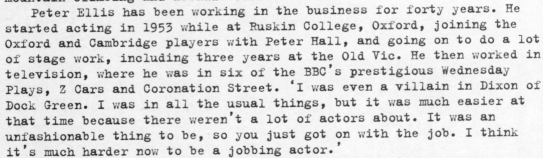

'The strange thing,' Ellis continues, 'is that when you meet the real senior officers in the Met, they are actually quite radical. They are the ones constantly pushing for change in the force. But I think Brownlow acts as he does because he is very much a politician. He'll go which ever way the current fashion indicates.'

Ellis would like to see more humour in Brownlow and hopes that the new, longer-format episodes will give his character the chance to grow. 'The half-hour episodes didn't allow the senior officers to get out much, but we're playing scenes out on location a lot more now.' He recently filmed an episode on Dartmoor, where the squad were on a mountain-climbing and assault-course exercise.

Peter Ellis has been working in the business for forty years. He started acting in 1953 while at Ruskin College, Oxford, joining the Oxford and Cambridge players with Peter Hall, and going on to do a lot of stage work, including three years at the Old Vic. He then worked in television, where he was in six of the BBC's prestigious Wednesday Plays, Z Cars and Coronation Street. 'I was even a villain in Dixon of Dock Green. I was in all the usual things, but it was much easier at that time because there weren't a lot of actors about. It was an unfashionable thing to be, so you just got on with the job. I think it's much harder now to be a jobbing actor.'

Ellis has three grown-up sons, and lived alone, quite content, he says, to potter about in his cottage at weekends or sail his boat until he took a few weeks off to do a play in Suffolk. 'I went up to Suffolk to do *Educating Rita* for two weeks and met Anita. She played the Julie Walters part, and I was the Professor. We've been together ever since, and eventually got married and have two children who are six and three.'

When he has spare time, Ellis directs documentaries and has also been involved in community arts since the sixties, working on a constant flow of projects to bring drama and new writing to young people. 'At the moment we are trying to set up an arts centre in the East End, and I'm doing a new writing event in a school in Brighton which has been under-performing.'

BEN ROBERTS plays

CH. INSPECTOR DEREK CONWAY

Ben Roberts, a trained engineer, became an actor twenty years ago, when his Bayswater landlord roped him into an ILEA drama class. Thoroughly enjoying himself, he dropped the engineering and managed to win a place as a mature student at the Webber Douglas Drama School in Kensington.

Working as an assistant stage manager, mainly shifting scenery, at a theatre festival in Scotland he met the love of his life Helen Lloyd, the leading lady in one of the productions. The couple now live in Nottingham, where Helen is a producer at Central Television. Roberts commutes on a weekly basis from their Ilkeston home to the south London house he rents with fellow Bill star Ray Ashcroft, who plays DS Daly.

Roberts sees Conway as a straightforward old-fashioned copper, whose organisational skills are second to none. Conway is also a highly trained negotiator, as seen in the recent hour-long Bill episode 'On Air', where he tracks down a rapist via a spot on local radio by appealing for information and witnesses. The rapist himself phones in and it is up to Conway to keep him talking and discover where the man is. Conway's main bone of contention at the moment is his desire for promotion, and this causes friction between him and Brownlow, who he believes is somehow responsible for holding him back.

Having met real chief inspectors in the course of his research for the role he has played for more than ten years, Roberts holds firmly to the belief that they do one of the toughest jobs in the force. He says he could never be a policeman himself. Instead, he has continued to practise his engineering skills alongside his acting career. A qualified pilot, he is building a biplane in his garage from a kit. 'My wife said I was mad when I told her what I wanted to do. But a friend in The Bill costume department told me he had read a newspaper article about these kit planes, and that there are now more than thirteen flying.'

Doggedly determined, and nurturing a glorious dream, he has spent over a year building the airframe and wings in his thirty-foot garage, and intends to import the engine from Australia. 'I have always been fascinated by First World War aircraft, and this is just like those early days of flying,' he says wistfully. 'It's like being able to take off and go wherever you like.'

ERIC RICHARD plays

SGT BOB CRYER

Tough but fair, Sergeant Bob Cryer is a reliable, dedicated old-school policeman who can see trouble coming. Like Dixon of Dock Green before him, he has been around for a lifetime. 'He is Sun Hill!' Actor Eric Richard, who has played the part of Cryer in The Bill since 1984, is emphatic. 'He's what the police officer in The Bill is really all about. Straight and fair. I always say about him, victim or villain you would best be dealt with by Cryer.'

Eric Richard, who did a lot of theatre work before joining the cast of The Bill, did not become an actor until his late twenties. At the time he was the father of two and running a successful motor accessories business in south London, but felt there was something missing in his life. Inspired by a friend he joined the local amateur dramatics society and soon realised that acting was what he wanted to do.

After training with the South London Theatre Centre in Norwood, Richard was cast in supporting roles in high-profile programmes like The Onedin Line, Angels and Juliet Bravo. He also appeared in the epic mini-series Shogun, starring Richard Chamberlain. The experience was not as glamorous as he had hoped, despite the vast budget and Far Eastern location. 'My character, a shipwrecked crew member captured by the Samurai, got gangrene in the end and rotted in a pit!' Though Sun Hill can often be a tricky place to work, luckily the character of Bob Cryer has never had to face anything quite so gruesome.

Richard thinks it would be a mistake to give The Bill a more domestic feel. It is many years since Cryer's wife Shirley and his problem son Patrick were last mentioned and he prefers to see his character's life from the perspective of the workplace. Up to autumn 1998, characters' lives outside the job had only been portrayed when they had a direct effect on their professional life. 'One of the Bill's strengths has been not worrying about who's doing what to whom in their private lives. I mean,' he laughs, 'the idea of Bob going off and having an affair with a probation officer just wouldn't be very entertaining. But I suppose you never know!'

In his private life, Richard is married to his second wife Tina, a teacher, and has a seven-year-old son, Jack, and a two-year-old daughter, Sophie. A motorbiking fanatic, he can often be seen striding about south London in his leathers, in striking contrast to the more sombre Cryer. The family have all become biking mad, and go on frequent invigorating holidays touring Europe by motorbike, with Jack strapped into a side-car or riding pillion.

COLIN TARRANT plays

INSPECTOR ANDREW MONROE

Actor Colin Tarrant feels he gets a rather restrained postbag, considering that the notably severe character of Inspector Andrew Monroe is not someone who courts popularity. 'I get letters saying he's an upright sort of bloke, not much sense of humour, that Monroe should smile more often. But they don't like it if I shout at someone. "You were very unkind to poor Quinnan", or Stamp, or Garfield, they reprimand.'

Tarrant, who has played the character of Monroe for nearly ten years, hopes he will continue to be the stern but fair and honest policeman who tries to do a difficult job as well as he can. At the same time, he hopes for more scope for humour in his character, and that Monroe will get out of his office more often.

Inspector Andrew Monroe, who began his working life as a miner, is still physically very tough indeed. A force to be reckoned with in the Sun Hill squad, he puts the fear of God into his superiors and subordinates alike. He is, above all, a tireless worker and a naturally meticulous man. Though he has had very little formal education, he has a flawless knowledge of police procedure and will, with great politeness, correct absolutely anyone who gets it wrong.

Though Monroe is in no way a cosy person, he has been happily married for twenty years and has two teenage daughters at home. Colin Tarrant, a Derbyshire man, who is far less severe than the character he plays, likes 'just knocking about, really', and lives alone, delighting in his eleven-year-old son Juma (an African name meaning 'warm-hearted'). They play a lot of football together and argue only because they support different teams. 'Unfortunately he supports Arsenal,' laughs Tarrant. 'I try to get him to support my team, Nottingham Forest!'

'CID' DCs

MARK WINGETT plays

DC JIM CARVER

'He's got a big streak of goodness running through him, James Carver,' says veteran Bill actor Mark Wingett, who has played the dependable Carver for sixteen years, with a generous grin as he sloshes foaming water over his new Range Rover with an enormous sponge. 'But it often gets him into trouble because he tends to follow his heart rather than stick to the rules.'

I caught Wingett, thirty-eight, for a precious few minutes while washing his car on The Bill's back lot. He is taking extra care of this latest vehicle, having recently written off its predecessor. Originally from Portsmouth, he is something of a water sports enthusiast and keeps a boat moored down in Littlehampton from which he fishes and scuba dives for old wrecks. The diving has become a big hobby, and was incorporated into an unusual episode of The Bill called 'Still Waters', in which Carver had to train somebody to dive. 'It all began to go wrong when she discovered a body on a motorbike at the bottom of the harbour,' says Wingett.

He has been living with his girlfriend, Jamaican film make-up artist Sharon Martin, for thirteen years, although they have never got round to marrying. He lights up when asked about their children. Sharon has a son, Benny, twenty, from a previous relationship, and the couple have a six-year-old daughter called Jamila, meaning 'beautiful' in Arabic. 'We were going to call her Jamila "Jehana", which means "beautiful goddess", but then we thought that would be too much!'

Carver, Wingett explains, originally wanted to be a traditional copper, wearing a uniform and dealing with the public. Enthused by Burnside, however, who once had a strong influence on him, Carver sold his soul to CID. Now he is back in uniform doing 'tenure' and, although this is considered a standard-procedure sideways move in the police service, Carver — as is often the case with real DCs in this position — sees it as a kick in the teeth. 'He doesn't like it that much, and starts to develop a drink problem,' continues Wingett, poker-faced as he narrowly misses dousing me with a water hose. 'He begins to do things a bit out of character, like sleeping with people he shouldn't, and he is blackmailed at one point.'

Having dedicated so many years to playing Jim Carver it is hardly surprising that Wingett is frequently mistaken for a real policeman. Once he was leaning against a car smoking a cigarette during a break in filming when a car containing four CID officers screeched to a halt beside him. 'They said they were going to report me for smoking on duty! When I told them I was an actor working for Thames Television, they said they were going to report the company for setting a bad example — and they did.'

KARL COLLINS plays

DC DANNY GLAZE

'Danny has worked hard to be a detective
and made a determined effort to fit into
what is after all a very white,
competitive male environment,' says actor
Karl Collins of the character he plays.
'He needs people to like him and has a
natural warmth coupled with a quick,
instinctive brain.'

DC Danny Glaze arrives at Sun Hill in
an episode entitled 'Makeover', which co-
incidentally is Jim Carver's first day
back in uniform. Glaze has to be doubly cautious and tactful, therefore,
as Carver doesn't find it easy to make the switch and Glaze has
effectively taken his post in CID.

Danny Glaze is a twenty-eight-year-old Londoner with seven years,
experience in the Metropolitan Police. The move to Sun Hill is his second
CID posting; he applied for the transfer with the aim of broadening his
experience. Having met DC Rawton on a recent course and liked what he
saw, Glaze thinks he will be comfortable with the Sun Hill CID. In fact,
Rawton's enthusiasm when she learns that he is to join the department
fuels the others' curiosity about him, but serves mainly to encourage a
degree of rivalry from the male team members.

'One or two of his colleagues are going to have a problem with

him, particularly DC Skase,' explains
Collins. 'And in spite of his even temper,
when pushed, Danny can really lose it and
it's best to run for cover when he does.'

Nottingham-born Karl Collins has had
plenty of television experience, including
roles in Casualty and Eastenders, and has
also played villain Everton Warwick over
several episodes of The Bill last year.
Collins is pleased with his new role on the
right side of the law. 'Being a regular
character in The Bill is a great opportunity
– especially as they let me keep my
distinctive hairstyle!' Collins said on
getting the part. 'When I get stopped in the
street, the kids shout, "Hey, Michael
Jackson!" or "Jackson 5!", while the adults
say, "Respect for the afro, brother."'

But the afro has proved too easily
recognisable on the Sun Hill estates for a CID
officer trying to blend in. 'Because of continuity and going under cover,
I get it trimmed regulary by Gustave Bjorkman at Vidal Sassoon.'

JOY BROOK plays

DC KERRY HOLMES

Scarborough-born Joy Brook admits to a delightful first day on The Bill due to a mix-up. 'One of the cast members hadn't turned on their alarm, or something. So instead of doing a huge complicated scene as my first ever scene in The Bill, I did a more intimate one-to-one scene with Russell Boulter. He's wonderful to work with as he's such a good actor. It was a lovely welcome.'

Brook, who trained at the Guildhall Drama School at London's Barbican Centre, never imagined she would be in The Bill. 'When I was at college I thought my acting career would be largely Shakespeare and the RSC, but now I'm doing lots of television. I'm having the best time tackling gun-toting robbers in bank vaults and getting into fist fights with prison inmates.'

She thinks Kerry Holmes is great: 'An interesting character to play because she is so ballsy! She's a good detective because she doesn't take no for an answer. Many of the younger male CID officers think she is a bit of a swot, but she's too confident to ever really allow the jibes to get to her and isn't slow at coming up with a quick riposte. And,' she smiles, 'Holmes also possesses a mischievous streak, asking questions of her senior colleagues that others wouldn't dare to and then playing the innocent.'

To date Brook has had starring roles in Peak Practice, Dalziel and Pascoe, and has played a 'nice girl', rather than a prostitute, in Band of Gold 2, which she says is the only job she has ever had where she has managed to keep her clothes on.

Of the controversial scene in 'Follow Through', in which DC Holmes, undercover in a woman's prison, is naked in the shower with a lesbian inmate, Brook explains: 'I did take my clothes off but by definition it couldn't be explicit because of the time it went out. The eroticism was all in the writing, which in that episode was very subtle. It was blown out of all proportion by the press.

'It was a fabulous episode for Holmes, and great for me to have to play a character in that kind of danger. I can't play nice characters – playing somebody with a bit of an edge is good!'

An enthusiast on all fronts – from her job to her roller-skating and the DIY she is carrying out on her new house – at twenty-nine, Brook knows her own mind. She intends to stay with The Bill as long as Holmes continues to get good storylines. 'As long as they write good things for her I want to play the part. I'm just not very good at being bored!'

GEORGE ROSSI plays

DC DUNCAN LENNOX

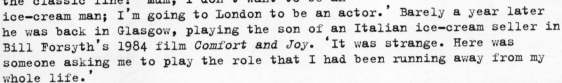

Thirty-seven-year-old George Rossi was in the bath with his young kids when he got the call from The Bill's executive producer Richard Handford to say he had got the part of DC Lennox. His partner, Welsh-born Catrin, handed him the phone: 'I just wanted to welcome you on board,' laughed Handford.

Rossi, from the famous Italian/Scottish ice-cream making family, remembers leaving home with the classic line: 'Mum, I don't want to be an ice-cream man; I'm going to London to be an actor.' Barely a year later he was back in Glasgow, playing the son of an Italian ice-cream seller in Bill Forsyth's 1984 film *Comfort and Joy*. 'It was strange. Here was someone asking me to play the role that I had been running away from my whole life.'

Since then Rossi has developed a taste for action, playing the part of Kevin for two years in the oil-rig drama Rough Necks. 'It was terrifying but brilliant,' he says, 'especially when we were filming in gales and hurricanes.' He has also appeared in other police drama such as Thieftakers, Taggart and Trial and Retribution, and so has some idea of what to expect from a copper. 'Lennox is a great character because he's really cheeky, and wears flash clothes, unlike the other detectives.'

A bulky Glaswegian with an ironic sense of humour, Lennox has enjoyed some quirky scripts since his arrival at Sun Hill in October 1998. His motives for a transfer from Epsom to the East End are a mystery to his colleagues in CID, until they discover in his first episode, 'The Fat Lady Sings', that it is Shona, his high-flying wife, who dictated the move. And that it is her salary which pays for their Docklands riverside apartment.

In Lennox's second episode, 'Team Work', DCI Meadows comically insists that Lennox complete a fitness course while simultaneously attempting to pursue a case, an episode that illustrates perfectly Lennox's ability to combine an air of profound laziness with sudden bursts of enthusiasm if he senses the chance of an arrest. There is nothing Lennox enjoys more than nicking a villain, and he takes even more pleasure in annoying his suspects by treating them with immense affability.

George Rossi spends a lot of time with his young family. 'The kids watch me on television and I think my little girl, Matilda, thinks I'm a real policeman sometimes.' But he tries not to talk about the show or run through his lines with Catrin. 'When you're really working in the business you don't want to talk about fiction all the time, you want to have a real life. I do DIY, I cook.'

When Rossi heard that Jack Nicholson had employed Harrison Ford to build his kitchen he was impressed. 'I thought, Great! I want to be like that. I don't want to spend my time networking down at Groucho's [the trendy media club in Soho]. I want to be a real person, at home.'

GREGORY DONALDSON plays

DC TOM PROCTOR

Twenty-five-year-old Gregory Donaldson,
who has played The Bill's DC Proctor for
the last two years, can also be heard late
at night on UK Rumble, the internet radio
station where he is a part-time DJ.
'Young, free and single', Hastings-born
Donaldson loves the fact that he can be
heard all over the world via the Net.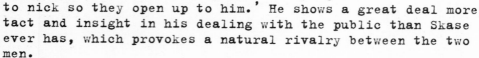

He is also enthusiastic about the
character of DC Tom Proctor. 'He's keen,
sharp and up to date on the law,' explains
Donaldson. 'He has a few run-ins with old-
school officers like Carver, and also puts
Skase's nose out of joint a bit as he
comes in as a younger officer. But,' he
emphasises, 'he's likeable and he actually
makes friends with the people he's trying
to nick so they open up to him.' He shows a great deal more
tact and insight in his dealing with the public than Skase
ever has, which provokes a natural rivalry between the two
men.

Donaldson left drama school four years ago, and swiftly
went into a run of the sell-out gay play *Something About Us*
by Andrew Alty at west London's Lyric Studio, which
received a lot of critical attention. He also starred in
Skin, a Channel 4 film about skinheads. He was thrilled to
gain the TV role of DC Proctor after very little television
experience. His only other TV appearances, apart from a
small part as a young policeman in Silent Witness 2, have
been playing villains on The Bill. 'I had two guest
appearances, one as a thief, the other as a thug!' he
laughs.

After two years of playing DC Proctor, Donaldson is
keen to see his character develop and have more of an edge.
'I'd like him to get more of a chip on his shoulder about
criminals, or a particular group of criminals. At the
moment I feel that Tom Proctor is a little bit too nice to
everyone. I want to make him more interesting!' he pleads
good-naturedly.

LIBBY DAVISON plays

DC LIZ RAWTON

Libby Davison commutes a regular 300 miles from her home in Newcastle to play the part of the dour Geordie DC Rawton. Despite it being a tough juggling act for the mother of two young children she has made a success of this no-nonsense role.

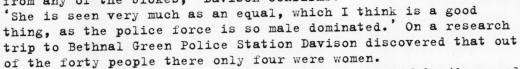

A strong personality herself, Davison enjoys playing the tough, independent Rawton. 'She doesn't take any nonsense from any of the blokes,' Davison confirms. 'She is seen very much as an equal, which I think is a good thing, as the police force is so male dominated.' On a research trip to Bethnal Green Police Station Davison discovered that out of the forty people there only four were women.

DC Liz Rawton, in her early thirties, is unfazed by the usual laddish routines around her. Her humour and guile are her best weapons. She joined CID at Sun Hill following a spell with SO11, criminal intelligence. There, she spent time honing her surveillance skills and experience in undercover operations, which tend to allow her to put criminals away using her brain rather than her brawn.

Davison first appeared in The Bill as a prostitute and then returned six months later as DC Rawton. The promised long television contract came as good news, as she had not done much TV work before. Apart from a small part in Byker Grove, Davison had worked mainly in theatre and as a club singer. She could not turn down the opportunity to do a concentrated time on television, though it meant leaving her husband Steve and children Billie, seven, and Liam, five, during the week.

'It's actually quite nice getting the train up on a Friday night because it gives me time to chill out. It is very hard to leave the children, but I talk to them every night on the phone and luckily I've got a brilliant nanny, so I don't need to worry.' Davison and her husband, who runs his own auto-electrical company, have been together for thirteen years. They met when she was working as a dental nurse and he came in as a patient. She claims to have besieged him with recall cards until she finally got his attention. 'At first he just thought I was a really bad receptionist!'

She prefers to bring up her children in her own home town, where they are surrounded by family and friends, rather than relocate to London. 'That support network is so important,' she says. Her favourite time of the week is the family Sunday lunch in Newcastle. 'My mam comes round and we cook the meal between us. It's usually chicken or lamb with roast potatoes. The children adore roast potatoes – they'd even eat them with porridge!'

IAIN FLETCHER plays

DC ROD SKASE

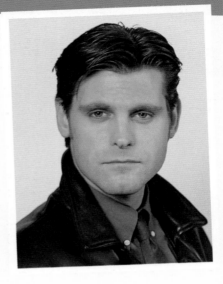

Insolent but suave, the smouldering DC Rod Skase is scared of nothing and no one. Tall and handsome, he towers above many of his Sun Hill colleagues and has the arrogance to match his stature. Generally, his intelligence and dedication to the job mean that he tends to get away with an offhand manner, but his attitude does not always endear him to his colleagues, some of whom do not trust him at all.

'Before I joined The Bill,' reveals actor Iain Fletcher, 'I was a total hippie. I had long hair, hardly ever shaved and spent my days playing the guitar and hanging out with friends. I'm still a hippie at heart, but having my hair cut to play DC Skase has given me a different perspective on life.'

Fletcher grew up in the sleepy seaside resort of Littlehampton, though he prefers to refer to it as the more exotic 'LA' – short for Little 'Ampton! The youngest of four brothers who were all encouraged to go into their father's engineering business, he veered away from the conventional and followed his heart to drama school. However, following graduation, he had a character-building eighteen months out of work before he got the call from The Bill. The part of the difficult, self-centred DC Skase, whom Fletcher has played for the last six years, was his first professional role.

He lives with his two Persian-cross cats, Butch Cassidy and Sundance Kid, in a Victorian terraced house in East Dulwich, conveniently near to The Bill set in Merton. Although he can cook, he never eats at home, and a girlfriend was once amused to find that the only item in his kitchen cupboard was a jar of lime marmalade. Instead, he dines either at The Bill's Bosun House canteen or at an assortment of favourite south-London restaurants. 'There are loads of good Indian restaurants where I live, and I love to hang out in clubs and listen to jazz and blues.'

With a mischievous smile, he claims to have frequent cock-ups on set. 'I've actually driven the CID car over one of the crew's feet!' He remembers the worst incident with an agonised look. He and Mark Wingett (DC Carver) were doing an episode where they were playing football for the Sun Hill team. 'When they stopped filming we were having a bit of a wrestle in the back of the goalmouth, and I broke one of my ribs and Mark dislocated his shoulder.'

DSs AND SENIOR OFFICERS

BILLY MURRAY plays

DS DON BEECH

East End boy Billy Murray, fifty-six, was close to the notorious Krays when he was growing up. 'What people don't understand,' says Murray, 'is that the Krays used to run London and, if you're in boxing, like I was, you couldn't fail to come across them.' He used to spar with Charlie Kray, who got him into the film extras' association. When Murray wanted to go to drama school and couldn't get a grant, Kray paid for his first year.

For twenty-five years, Murray spent his career playing roles on both sides of the law in hit shows like The Sweeney, Minder, Casualty and EastEnders, he was also supergrass Joey Davis in the gangster movie *McVicar* with Roger Daltrey, and a heavy in *Performance* with Mick Jagger. Now as DS Beech in The Bill since January 1995 he has become a household name.

He both adores and identifies with the character he plays. 'Beech is a maverick who does things his own way and gets results. But it's not all hard-boiled detective work for him – he loves a gamble and has got an eye for the women too.' Beech tends to sail close to the wind, and his colleagues sometimes question his behaviour. But, over his time in the job, he has made good contacts with senior officers and villains alike. He refuses to seek approval for his choice of friends and is in no way afraid of the disapproval of his colleagues and superiors. Remarkably similar, then, to the twinkly-eyed actor who plays him.

Murray is a family man, and lives with his wife Elaine, an ex-Bunny Girl, in a stunning former gamekeeper's cottage outside Brentwood in Essex. He has a boy and a girl in their twenties from his first marriage, and two daughters with Elaine. Recently he faced up to a tough ordeal in his private life. Defending his fifteen-year-old daughter from a drug dealer last year, he was arrested and accused of assault. Completely exonerated by the jury after a nerve-wracking trial, he received hundreds of letters from parents who congratulated him on trying to protect his child from drugs. 'I wanted it to go to court,' Murray says seriously. 'I'd told those men, "You don't want to mess with me because I'll become your worst nightmare."'

When not filming The Bill, Murray likes to unwind by gardening. 'I started gardening out of sheer necessity,' he concedes. 'We were practically overrun by a mass of rhododendrons, tall cypress hedges, roses and camellias. I'd never used a lawnmower before. Now I have seven, and I study my lines while I'm sitting on one cutting the grass!'

RUSSELL BOULTER plays

DS JOHN BOULTON

'He's a ruthless guy with a vicious streak, a bad good-guy who breaks the rules to get results,' says actor Russell Boulter of the complex character of DS Boulton. 'But if you're in the wrong, he's the last person you want to see. He's the kind of cop you'd want on your side.'

Liverpool-born Boulter left drama school in 1984 and went straight in to the Royal Shakespeare Company where he understudied forty-seven parts in two seasons. With a strong singing voice he went on to work in musicals, playing Mick in *Blood Brothers* in the West End and Joey in *Pal Joey* at the Bristol Old Vic. Soon Boulter was inundated with TV work, quickly becoming known as an inspector in Heartbeat, a gay character in Carla Lane's Luv and Primrose's poet boyfriend in The Darling Buds of May, before joining the cast of The Bill.

His first appearance was at the end of 1993. In a two-hander with DC Carver (an episode in which two main characters are focused on), Boulton was introduced as a character whose partner had recently been killed in a drugs bust. Psychologically disturbed by the ordeal, he had turned into a kind of vigilante policeman. In the episode, 'Faith in the System', Boulton beats up a man who he thinks has attacked a pensioner and then expects a horrified Carver to turn a blind eye, which, of course, he doesn't.

'Boulton would deliberately go further than was necessary because he was taking some kind of personal satisfaction in hurting people he perceived to be villains. You never quite know whether he is corrupt, though it appears he is not, but he is a bit out of control,' Boulter says of the volatile Boulton.

Approached three times to join the cast of The Bill on a full-time basis, Boulter finally acquiesced in September 1995.

Boulter is a keen amateur photographer and enjoys taking candid shots of life behind the scenes at The Bill. While would-be cast members await their auditions in the Castings Department, they can take in the atmosphere reflected in a permanent exhibition of Russell's work.

RAY ASHCROFT plays

DS GEOFF DALY

Down-to-earth Northerner Ray Ashcroft likes being in a long-term television show: 'It's the most ambient situation for an actor to have,' he emphasises. Having played DS Daly for the last three years, it is not just the quality of the programme he appreciates, but also the people who create such a pleasant atmosphere to work in. Ashcroft, from a working-class background in Sheffield, abhors pretentiousness. 'It's not theatrical, there are no brow-moppers here. If there were I wouldn't have survived as long!' The jobs he has most disliked have been the ones with, as he puts it, a 'luvvie' cast.

He fell into the profession at seventeen when a cast member dropped out of a student production being run by a friend and he was asked to fill in at short notice. Since then he has worked consistently, training in local theatre and going on to work in television and film. Before The Bill he played policemen in The Chief, Emmerdale, Hetty Wainthrop Investigates, Chandler and Co the list goes on. 'My joke is,' he grins, 'that once you get into your forties we all start looking like the same person anyway, and that person happens to be a policeman.'

Originally Ashcroft was cast as a villain in The Bill and then, in 1993, put in a brief appearance as the racist PC Rob Leach. 'Totally ironic for me,' he confides, 'as my partner is black and my kids are mixed race.'

DS Daly, the enthusiastic Yorkshireman with the wry sense of humour, the role he has played since June 1996, is quite different. 'Daly is a gentle and sensitive guy who thinks things out,' explains Ashcroft. 'His sensitivity can be very useful when it comes to eliciting information from people. But Daly can also be tough when he needs to be and is not easily ruffled.'

Ashcroft plays for The Bill football team and jogs to work every morning from his nearby house, which he shares during the week with fellow cast member Ben Roberts. He tells me with amusement that his health kick has more to do with vanity and combating his beer consumption than the more obvious motivation of keeping in trim to play a policeman.

Research with real police at Bethnal Green showed Ashcroft what a difficult job law enforcement actually is, and he confesses he could never be a real-life policeman. He is, however, quite happy to continue acting the part behind the cameras. 'It's a great show and I've got a great job. But one of the best things about it is that I get Saturdays off so I can go back home and watch Sheffield United play!'

SHAUN SCOTT plays

DI CHRIS DEAKIN

Dashing Detective Inspector Deakin joined the squad at Sun Hill five years ago when he was thrown out of the Flying Squad and forced to suffer the indignity of being disciplined by demotion because of his affair with a senior officer's wife. He is a policeman of the old school and would never break the rules, though he is prepared to take chances if he thinks he will get a result. Dedicated to his job, he is by no stretch of the imagination a 'bent' copper, but greatly resents the paperwork that ties up all the loose ends.

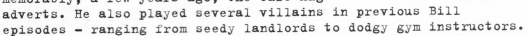

Deakin is played by Canadian-born public schoolboy Shaun Scott, who was brought up in Northern Ireland and then Dorset by his mother, a nurse, when his father left to return to Canada when Scott was only two years old. He trained at RADA and got his first acting break in Dublin alongside Liam Neeson and Stephen Rea, but then struggled for some years before winning television roles in *A Month in the Country*, Brass and, memorably, a few years ago, the Café Hag adverts. He also played several villains in previous Bill episodes – ranging from seedy landlords to dodgy gym instructors.

Scott, forty-four, gained strength from his wife Caroline, who manages a Kensington restaurant, during a recent brush with throat cancer. 'I couldn't have coped without Caroline,' he confides, 'and I love her to bits.' He is also extremely proud of his teenage son, Alex, from a previous relationship, and values the time they spend together at weekends.

Not content merely to endanger his life grappling with villains on The Bill, Scott is also a keen amateur racing driver. Taking his 2.8-litre Mercedes on to the track with fifty others at Goodwood to raise money for Cancer Research, he took a bend at seventy mph causing the car to somersault. The car landed on its roof, smashing the windows, bonnet and sides. An ambulance arrived, but Scott and his passenger scrambled free unharmed. A shaken Scott surveyed the wreck, commenting, 'The main thing is no one was hurt, but I don't know what my wife is going to say!'

SIMON ROUSE plays

DCI JACK MEADOWS

'People are often surprised when they meet
me,' confides Simon Rouse, with a twinkle in
his eye. 'They expect me to be a lot harder
than I am, as Meadows is such a tough
policeman.'

Rouse has played The Bill's DCI Jack
Meadows since 1992. Meadows was a thoroughly
seasoned policeman when he joined CID at Sun Hill. An ex-superintendent for
AMIP (Area Major Incident Pool), he had worked on a number of cases in
conjunction with detectives at Sun Hill before being brought in to run the
show over the head of an initially resentful Frank Burnside.

'They wanted someone to come in and beat CID up, so I had to be very hard.
Over the years I've tried to mellow him a bit, make him less tense, but he
does have a strong presence.'

Playing Meadows for such a long stint, Rouse has learnt that you do not
have to play authority: 'You just assume it,' he explains. 'It's taken me
quite a long time to understand that because actors aren't naturally good at
authority. They tend to be chancers. Actors aren't like policemen, they're
much more fluid and have more diverse interests.'

Since August 1998, Rouse has found working on the longer episodes much
more fulfilling than the quick half-hour programmes in which he had begun to
feel his character was no longer developing. He particularly liked the
February 1999 episode, 'Slinging Mud', in which Meadows faced corruption
charges. 'Meadows is accused of taking a bribe when a wad of notes, totalling
5,000, is found under a desk in his department.' Rumours fly when it is
remembered that Meadows arrived at Sun Hill because he was demoted at his last
station following a corruption case; though the truth is that he was only
actually demoted from Superintendent because of his lack of supervision. In
'Slinging Mud', Meadows has the chance to send down a notorious villain who
fights dirty, conspiring to make Sun Hill CID and Meadows in particular look
corrupt by pleading false evidence, and it is some time before Meadows's name
is cleared. Rouse found the demands on his character a welcome challenge: 'I
got very worried. I had an emotional journey to make.'

During the course of an investigation, Meadows recently travelled to
France. There he met a beautiful woman, the manager of the hotel at which he
was staying in Normandy, and had an affair. It was a chance to see the hard
man get in touch with his sexuality, even showing that he has a heart.

A Yorkshireman, Rouse is the son of an Inspector of Education who wanted
him to go to university. Instead he won a scholarship to the Rose Bruford
Drama School and became an actor. He has since worked extensively on the stage
and on both the large and small screens, memorably appearing in the film
Sheppy with Bob Hoskins in 1979, and playing a villain in the long-running TV
hit comedy Bread. He met his wife, the former actress Annie Holloway when they
were both at Stratford with the Royal Shakespeare Company. 'She is now a
painter,' he tells me proudly, pointing across his dressing room to a splendid
oil painting that he says is one of her early works.

It is a rather well-executed nude of Rouse himself. He is charming, but he
is definitely not shy.

OCCASIONAL AND NEW CHARACTERS

CHRISTOPHER ELLISON plays

DCI FRANK BURNSIDE

Sun Hill's hardest cop, the mean, moody and magnificent DCI Frank Burnside rejoined the cast of The Bill in October 1998 in an episode entitled 'Cast No Shadow', primed to strike terror into the hearts of every East End villain.

Christopher Ellison, who has been busy in his time away from Sun Hill guest starring in such shows as Crime Traveller and Birds of a Feather, was pleased to step back into the character of Burnside after five years away, though he admits to having to watch some of the old episodes to remind himself what Burnside was really like – and he hasn't changed. 'The public wouldn't accept him as a softy. He was always a bit of a loner, and you never knew much about his life outside the nick. Though of course he is a bit of a ladies' man,' Ellison smiles, 'that is kept very much under wraps – he's probably been having a long-standing affair.

'Secrets,' Ellison reveals, 'are the key to Burnside's character; he's very much a man of mystery.'

Ellison confesses that he has always found it more interesting to play the baddy, and though Burnside is not exactly that, he enjoys the fact that the character has a bit of an edge to him. 'I certainly wouldn't like to cross a guy like DCI Burnside,' he continues. 'After all, he's renowned for putting suspects' heads down toilets and calling them rather choice names!'

CAROLINE CATZ plays

DS (formerly PC) Rosie Fox

'I jumped at the chance to come back,' says actress Caroline Catz who played PC Rosie Fox at Sun Hill over several weeks in autumn 1998. Following persistent sexual harassment, culminating in near rape by obsessed PC Eddie Santini on a locker room floor, Fox requested a transfer. Now the tormented policewoman is back at Sun Hill, a sergeant in the Murder Squad, and it is her job to see that Santini gets his comeuppance. 'Everyone wanted to see Rosie and Santini together again,' reveals Catz. 'When I walked in, it was like I'd never been away.'

The sexual chemistry between the characters provoked a remarkable audience reaction, which Catz was astonished by. 'People pointed me out in the street to their friends. They'd talk about me as though I wasn't there.'

Men called out to her: 'You all right Rosie?', and told her in no uncertain terms what they would like to do to Santini. In some ways she is relieved by this response: 'I'm so glad men seem to be on Rosie's side. I was afraid they would think what he did was okay, and macho.' Following the initial episodes Catz received letters from women who had been sexually harassed at work, including two policewomen, glad that the subject was being aired. Despite this Catz herself believes that many women find Santini attractive, 'He's charismatic, he's a conman. And many women are attracted to rogues.'

Unlike the confident, organised, more up-front DS Fox, Catz describes herself as shy and chaotic. Recently cast as PC Cheryl Hutchins in ITV's police drama The Vice, Catz found herself thrust into the world of Soho peep shows to research the role. 'I was so naive,' she confesses. 'I couldn't believe the things I saw. Some of those sex aids — I certainly wouldn't know what to do with them!'

ALEX WALKINSHAW plays

PC DALE SMITH

Twenty-four-year-old Essex boy Alex Walkinshaw plays wild PC
Dale Smith, who arrives at Sun Hill
looking for action following a rather
dull posting in a quiet leafy suburb.

An ex-squaddie, Smith is a Londoner
from a large dysfunctional family. He
hated school, learning to look after
himself because he had to, and leaving
as soon as he could. Escaping into the
army, he enjoyed life as one of the
lads, with more than his fair share of
drunken late nights, gratuitous sex, and
silly wind-ups.

Smith has now served as a police
officer for three years and is immensely
brave, though he can be stubborn and
opinionated. He is immediately accepted
on the Sun Hill relief, perceived as
'someone who will watch your back',
though someone like Monroe might
describe him as reckless.

Known for his single-mindedness, he will not suffer fools
or mince his words. He can sometimes be infuriating as he
often has more time for the local villain than he has for
somebody he thinks is a loser – as PC Luke Ashton discovers to
his cost.

Dedicated to his job, and one of the lads from the word go,
Smith can be narrow-minded. He is a sexist, and possibly even
a racist, and many people do not warm to him.

Actor Alex Walkinshaw is best known for his role as DS
Small in McCallum. He attended The Sylvia Young Theatre School
from the age of thirteen, and as a teenager had three previous
roles in The Bill – and was arrested on all three occasions.
Alex is a keen swimmer, at one time swimming butterfly for
Essex in competitions throughout Europe. Now he plays golf and
snooker and is an armchair football enthusiast. To his
amusement and perhaps a little to his chagrin he is widely
recognised from the Persil washing powder advertisement in
which he played a young man who goes for a job interview and
comes out successful but with his shirt hanging out of his
trousers.

Sun Hill Trivia

Programme making is littered with exotic facts and secrets, pratfalls and surreptitious dalliances: from the revelation that the actors who play the acrimonious Fox and Santini are really great friends to the little-known fact that PC Polly Page once spent an entire day filming in uniform with a pair of gold fluffy slippers on her feet – the only thing that could be found to fit her after she had suffered a sprained ankle. Here are a few useful nuggets of information.

- **Every year approximately 60,000 fan cards are given out to fans**

- **When filming on location, The Bill does not have permission to use sirens – so they are added in the dubbing suite**

- **Every night before a filming day, The Bill's cone man cones off the areas needed for the next day – to keep away unwanted traffic**

- **When John Major was prime minister he once requested several episodes of The Bill for Christmas viewing at his Chequers residence**

- **Metropolitan Police surveys show that the public gets most of its information about police work from The Bill**

- **There have been three versions of the 'walking feet' which used to form the show's closing credits: the same actress, Karen England, appeared in all three, while Paul Page-Hanson's size nines have appeared twice**

- **Peter Dean, who played Pete Beale in EastEnders for many years, was a sergeant in The Bill's pilot programme Woodentop**

- **In the early days the executive producer's office doubled as Chief Supt. Brownlow's office, and the canteen was used both as a set for the programme and by the cast and crew to eat in**

- **Geoff McQueen named 'Sun Hill' after a street in his home town of Royston, Hertfordshire**

- **The wardrobe department can often be seen 'distressing' new clothes with a cheese grater**

- **The 'heavy sounding' cell doors are actually made of plywood**

At the end of a long day, director Pip Broughton rehearses another shot in the underground garages with her back-ups in continuity, make-up and costume.

Each one-hour episode of The Bill involves four weeks of preparation, a two-week shoot, and two weeks of post-production editing. With three film units – colour-coded red, green and blue – working to record three episodes at any one time, it is a massive operation requiring precision scheduling in order for the large production team to do their jobs properly.

The shooting schedule is planned so that the three units can film at the same time. Often the actors are required to work on more than one episode in a week, which means keeping abreast of several different scripts simultaneously. At a particularly busy time for the show, when extra episodes are requested by the

network, additional freelance production crew are hired, linked to an existing unit and called a 'stripe'. Libby Davison, who plays DC Rawton, confides that she has recently worked on five different episodes in the same week!

The nervous PCs line up for a first take of their entry into the drugs den. Director Pip Broughton explains to the actors what she requires from this particular shot.

'Go, go, go ...' On a signal from DC Lennox an intrepid line-up of Boyden, Quinnan, Garfield, Stamp, Monroe, Hagen and McCann force open the metal mesh gates with a decisive smash of the heavy red police 'enforcer'. They storm in to raid drug dealers occupying the disused car park beneath a south-London council estate.

'Police, stay where you are!' shout the team as they thunder in, their flashing torches cutting through the eerily blue-lit darkness, their truncheons at the ready, primed to grab the nearest villain.

'And, cut ... thank you everybody,' calls first assistant Mike Purcell. 'Now, let's do it again ...'

I had arrived much earlier in the day and found myself on what seemed to be a typical Bill location. The vast greying estate, with its many film-friendly walkways and sprawling waste areas looked familiar from many a small-screen crime scene. I parked cautiously, as directed by location manager Richard Godfrey, alongside some adjacent houses and beneath a sign warning 'Beware of the Rottweiler'. A team from a security firm was installing metal spikes on top of a nearby wall.

Fact and fiction seemed to merge confusingly.

Walking round to the set, past the catering trucks

Location coners do the all-important job of clearing the roads of unwanted vehicles before The Bill team can start their day.

where the kitchen staff were preparing to provide meals on site for fifty, Richard Godfrey introduced me to his crucial team of 'coners' who had been at the location since early morning, putting out cones to clear space for the many necessary vehicles for props, electricals, cameras and catering. They were accompanied by the estate caretaker, an earnest young man with a mobile phone pressed importantly to his ear, hired by The Bill to liaise with the local residents for the duration of the shoot.

The entrance to the garage itself, concealed behind vast metal communal rubbish bins, was filthy and reeked of urine. I went in gingerly, stepping over the many electrical cables and tracks that were being arranged around the place, to see what the set designer had made of the grim interior. Magically, a

dealer's den had been constructed at the back of the low-ceilinged garages that stretch the considerable length of the building. A single bay, lit by dozens of flickering candles, stood out in the dusty, dank darkness, transformed to set the scene for the drugs raid.

Director Pip Broughton, who has fifteen years of directing in the theatre under her belt and more recently has directed two feature-length films for Channel 4, explained that this scene was to be one of the last in an episode entitled 'Out and About'. The episode concentrates on PC Quinnan who has been in hospital and near death following an attack by a gang of youths. Though physically fit again, he is still quite traumatised and suffering from post-traumatic stress disorder. He is now back on the beat, but is having problems functioning fully. At the end of a

Director Pip Broughton explains to the actors how she will line them up for maximum effect.

In the underground garages, drug dealers lurk inside the fantasy candle-lit den while the first assistant director Mike Purcell stands in for a camera rehearsal.

difficult day, Sgt Boyden suggests that Quinnan join him on a drugs raid to prove himself. Quinnan takes up the challenge.

'It's a medium-sized raid,' Broughton continues: 'heroin dealers that they've been informed about. It's quite well organised. What I've tried to do is shoot in a very real way so that we feel we're experiencing it, and can see from Quinnan's point of view that he is quite disorientated and really doesn't know what to do. That's why I'm covering it with quite a lot of shots and quite a lot of chaos and noise.'

Later in the evening they are to film shots of Quinnan saving one of his colleagues in the raid. He has not 'bottled out' at all and his confidence is restored, giving the story a positive, life-affirming conclusion.

It is the experienced first assistant director who appears to be running the floor, instructing the camera crew to 'turn over' and start the camera rolling, calling out 'action' to the actors and, finally, 'cut'. The crux of the director's job, Broughton reveals, is in the planning. 'There isn't time for me to do a lot of detailed re-working of the script on the "floor" because we have to shoot very fast. Every decision that you make in the four weeks of pre-production is really what makes it work on the day of shooting.'

The choice of location is important, together with the casting and the order of the schedule. Four weeks' work is put into preparing for the actual moment when a scene is shot. It is only then that the team are able to tackle the filming confidently.

'Today,' Broughton points out, 'it is quite difficult

for people to work in there because it's dusty and generally pretty unpleasant. You've got to try and keep people's morale up and make them believe in what they are doing.'

Recalling the last time she directed an episode of The Bill she smiles ruefully. 'I was seven and a half months pregnant, and standing all night on a night-shoot in the cold and the pouring rain. I began to panic that I would have it prematurely. Then an actor came up to me and said, "I'm really cold and really tired, but I can't complain because you're still standing there and you're seven and a half months pregnant!"'

Broughton intends to give this scene a particular look with the lighting and camera work, choosing deep blue lights to make it look like night, and also to create a confused effect to echo the disorientated feeling of the traumatised central character, Quinnan. The camera is to be hand-held, cameraman Graham Geddes balancing the camera on his shoulder and able to move freely with it. In contrast to this scene, most of the episode has been shot with

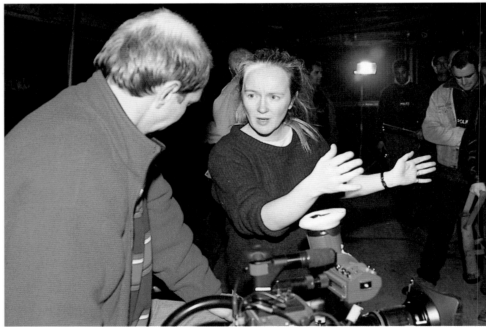

the camera static, or with very controlled-floor-to camera movement. 'I made a conscious decision to change style here because this is much more fast moving and emotional,' Broughton explains.

In her repeated filming of the same sequence, Broughton is aiming to have enough shots to be able to cut very quickly between them in the cutting room.

By using a montage of four shots to get the policemen through the gates, rather than have them simply storm through once, a rhythm is built up that creates a stronger dramatic effect – like a piece of music in pictures.

'I've got to take lots and lots of shots, and to vary my shot size. We're doing it so that there's a close-up

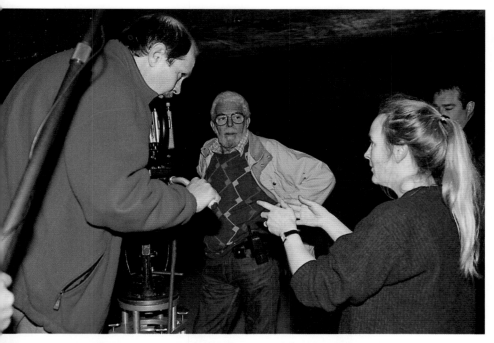

The cameraman, first assistant and director work out the complex camera angles for the shots required.

The Bill's extraordinary production schedule not only poses a problem for the scheduler, Nigel Wilson, but also keeps The Bill's two full-time police advisers very busy.

Both retired policemen, who between them boast fifty years of service in the Metropolitan Police, Trevor Hermes and Malcolm Haddow now work with writers, script editors and producers from the earliest premise stage, through to the storylines and scripts. From the start they discuss new ideas suggested by the writers, and mention themes which have been suggested to them by real police public affairs representatives who take an interest in keeping The Bill up to date with what is happening in the job. With over a hundred writers on the programme all hungry for ideas and insights, and the necessity of reading the scripts at every stage, the task of the police adviser is

and then a wide shot because the rhythm only works if you're varying the shots and cutting them together.

'The first shot I did, where I focused on the faces, was to build up the suspense because they are nervous. They know that there is a weak member of the team. The idea is for the viewer to have the same experience as the characters – that's always my mission!'

considerable. 'We're there,' says Trevor Hermes good-naturedly, 'to make sure that at every stage the text is accurate in terms of procedure, and that the police would react in the specified ways.'

One or other of the pair maintains a constant presence on location shoots. Today, assigned to the red unit, Hermes is controlling the use of the 'enforcer', a 36 lb red battering ram – rather like a fire-extinguisher in appearance – that in reality would only be used by a specially trained officer. He jokes that if they were using the real thing, instead of the prop which only weighs 18 lb, actor Tony O'Callaghan, who plays Sgt Boyden, probably would not even be able to lift it. 'If they're using handcuffs, if they're using the enforcer to break through the gates, or if they are using C.S. spray and asps [the new batons] I'm there to make sure that they look right.'

So much research and cross-checking of procedure goes into an episode before it gets to the production stage that rarely does anything go awry – any problems are dealt with earlier on. But with 80 per cent of The Bill now filmed on location it would be remarkable if there was never a hiccup. Hermes recalls one tricky incident, when a stabbing took place on the estate where they were filming. 'The police tried to blame the incident on our presence, though it had nothing to do with us. We had even broken for lunch when it occurred. In fact, we actually assisted with the arrest of a suspect. But an Inspector got out of his pram and said that if we hadn't been there it wouldn't have happened, which is totally wrong.

'Basically, the system prevents us from getting into

Police adviser Trevor Hermes.
Right: **In the drugs raid, PC Stamp uses considerable force to arrest a suspect.**

trouble – the police have got to clear us being here in the first place, and the council. They know why we are here, they know what we do. The Bill is such a big machine, and works so successfully that we should never have any problems.'

Between takes, the actors stagger out from the dusty atmosphere of the garage and sit on the open rear of a props van sipping tea from Styrofoam cups provided by the company tea wagon. They cheerfully sign autographs for an increasingly lively gaggle of local kids who are thrilled to meet the TV stars.

Graham Cole, who plays the dependable PC Stamp, leans against a wall in full uniform, his flat-topped blue hat slightly askew as he sips his tea and takes in the local ambience. Cole confesses to enjoying spending so much time out in the real world of the London streets, and does not think he would still be at The Bill after eleven years if the programme was studio based.

'There's a lot of liaison with the real boys, especially on this kind of estate,' he points out, 'because if they're doing low-key policing one thing you don't want to do is swamp the place with a bunch of look-a-like coppers! There's also a lot of liaison that goes on so that we don't upset the locals too much. But most of the time being out here is good fun, and people are good natured. The kids come running over to you and say things like, "My Mum really fancies you," which is a bit strange.' He throws back his head and roars with laughter. 'What am I supposed to say to that?'

A van and an observation – 'obbo' – car are parked further down the road and Action Vehicles co-ordinator Simon Mohun-Smith, who is in charge of the vehicles that go out on location, explains that there are no actual marked police cars being used today. However, when a car chase is called for there is often a great need for the villain to do some specialist driving. Mohun-Smith will supervise and explain what is needed of the stunt double for taking bends at break neck speed. Last week, he tells me, he worked with the getaway car villain in a thrilling three-minute sequence.

The Bill has a fleet of thirty-two action vehicles that are exact replicas of police cars, the only difference being that some of the cars are elongated like a van in order to hold a camera. They are not allowed to show the police markings when the cars are being driven to locations and the blue lights must be covered with masking tape. A code on the roof is there to identify them as dummies to real police helicopters. The sirens are not allowed to be used during filming on the streets, and the sound is only added later in the dubbing suite.

Above: **Actress Samantha Robson takes a new perspective on the scene.**
Opposite top: **Outside the dismal garages, actor Colin Tarrant takes a well-earned coffee break.**
Opposite bottom: **Make-up is constantly re-applied on set with the wear and tear of the long filming day.**

By now it is late and Samantha Robson, PC Hagen, stands shivering in the growing gloom while a make-up artist carefully checks her face, gently applying powder to a shiny nose. She is dressed in an uncomfortable stab jacket for the raid, and a passing costume assistant – weighed down by an armload of blue jackets – explains that the police uniforms are all the real thing, except for these foam-filled stab vests and the heavy overcoats they wear on the beat which are made of a special film-friendly fabric that makes no noise.

After hours on the set everyone is weary, grimy and cold, and the stench of the garages seems, if possible, to have become even more pungent. A hot meal break is coming up and an exhausted Robson asks a busy second assistant if she can go back to the unit base. A call through his walkie talkie confirms that she can, but even in the darkness her way is barred by yet more fans pleading for autographs. She signs a few with a smile, and then looks over at me for escape. 'I've got to do an interview now,' she excuses herself, threading her arm firmly through mine. 'I'll be back here soon to sign more.'

With the air of conspirators we stagger back along the perimeter of the estate in search of the kitchen truck and actors' Winnebago.

'Your life is so glamorous,' I remark.

Startled, she looks round at me. 'For a minute I thought you were serious.'

Above: **Stamp, McCann and Boyden relax in the discreet luxury of the actors' Winnebago.**
Right: **Many young fans are keen to meet their police idols from The Bill, and the cast enjoy their presence.**

Bill Brawls

TV policemen have come a long way since Dixon of Dock Green – when all it took to keep the great British public in line was a cheery 'Evenin' all' from the friendly local bobby. The urban environment now seems a much more violent place in which to live and television informs our perception of our society more forcefully. Realism is the order of the day, and reflecting the frequent necessity for the police to exert brute force is a crucial part of portraying real life in any police drama.

When police rush into a danger zone on a drugs raid, or are in pursuit of a dangerous criminal, they must protect themselves by immediately taking control of a situation. The Bill is at the forefront of showing policing as it really is.

Adrenaline often runs high on the Sun Hill relief and tempers can fray when an officer makes an unpopular decision or even inadvertently causes another officer to be injured. When blame is apportioned, it is sometimes not only the villains who have to be restrained when the men and women are pushed to their limits of endurance and forced to face the Judas within.

In a misunderstanding involving CID following a villain to Manchester, Carver is forced to defend his former boss Burnside, now working undercover.

Never the best of friends! Wily East End cop Beech gives the 'by-the-book' Northerner 'farmer' Daly a hard time.

Sgt Boyden is forced to separate two warring officers when Boulton has the temerity to suggest that the attack on Quinnan was his own fault

On a drugs raid in 'Out and About', PCs McCann and Garfield restrain and arrest a suspected drug dealer.

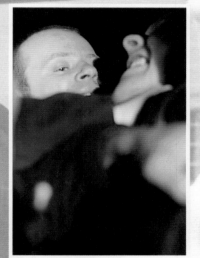

Quinnan warns Santini to back off.

During a shoot-out in 'Betrayal', Burnside's lover wrestles for control of the gun.

PC Quinnan is set upon by youths

PC Santini forces himself on PC Fox.

CHAPTER FOUR

BANGED UP

Originally conceived as an hour-long drama, The Bill was first broadcast in 1983. With its increasing popularity it went twice-weekly, and then became a half-hour thrice-weekly, almost 'soap' style format. Since August 1998 The Bill has run two nights a week on ITV, once again in an hour-long format.

'Banged Up' gives a digest of the episodes that tell the story of The Bill at Sun Hill over the course of nine months, from August 1998 to May 1999. The serious issues grappled with by the Sun Hill police force – from drug dealers to murderous paedophile

gangs, from burglaries to abductions – are followed by an audience of millions who focus with rapt attention on our guardians in blue.

'Deep End' 25 AUGUST 1998

written by Elizabeth-Anne Wheal directed by Ian White

When the body of a young junkie is found washed up on the banks of the Thames, DC Rawton suggests that PC Santini and his partner PC Fox, who is new to Sun Hill, work together to find out how the body got there. But, locked in disagreement over another case and exchanging harsh words over their differing sympathies, it is clear there is a problem within the partnership that may hinder their work.

Attracted to Fox, and arrogantly convinced that all women find him attractive, Santini seethes with jealousy when she goes undercover as a prostitute to help investigate the case for a joint CID and Drug Squad operation, necessarily dressing for the job in an overtly sexy dress. Santini is determined that she will be his next sexual conquest.

Eventually CID get their man, despite Santini nearly blowing the operation. There is a big celebration at Sun Hill and, after some goading by their fellow officers, Fox and Santini enjoy a drunken kiss. But things end on a darker note when minutes later Santini forces himself on Fox in the locker room, ignoring her pleas for him to stop. Suddenly, he is distracted by a noise and stops – but the damage has been done and Fox is left frightened and angry.

The gripping ninety-minute episode teams up PC Eddie Santini with new partner PC Rosie Fox, with whom his attachment becomes more than just professional.

'The Party's Over' 27 AUGUST 1998
written by Neil Clarke directed by Jo Johnson

PC Santini refuses to believe that his advances to PC Fox are unwelcome, inventing ways to work alongside her and permit proximity that she would rather do without. When he arrives on her doorstep with wine and flowers she recognises he is obsessed with her and takes the matter to the Police Federation Representative.

Meanwhile, DCs Skase and Proctor have to deal with a man who has previously helped them by providing an observation room for a drugs enquiry, but who has now developed a taste for the attention he has formerly enjoyed. When he complains of a prowler it soon becomes clear that he is a fantasist with a tendency to exaggerate.

'Bang, Bang, You're Dead'
28 AUGUST 1998
written by Elizabeth-Anne Wheal
directed by Paul Murton

The Sun Hill squad play a charity paintball game. It is a big day out for all of them, and on the bus Chief Inspector Conway and Inspector Monroe discuss strategy, while CID lay bets on the outcome. They draw lots for team leader, and PC Hollis wins. Conway is furious at having to take orders from the Sun Hill clown.

Although PC Santini has managed to persuade PC Fox that his intentions are honourable and professional, he still cannot keep his hands off her at the game. He shoots at her, using the cover of messy paint and general chaos to attempt to get intimate. Fox later asks Sgt Ackland if she can avoid partnering Santini for a while. But Ackland is unsympathetic, suggesting Fox should sort out her personal problems in her own time.

Top: **PC Fox rebuffs PC Santini's advances.**
Left: **Keen strategist Chief Inspector Conway, taking part in a charity paintball game.**

'Team Spirit' 1 SEPTEMBER 1998
written by Elizabeth-Anne Wheal
directed by Albert Barber

After weeks of torment, PC Fox finally decides to make an allegation of sexual assault against PC Santini, but finds herself isolated and without support. Most of the Sun Hill team side with Santini.

Fox tells her side of the story – the drunken kiss and the locker room assault – to DCI Meadows. Meadows does not feel able to proceed on the strength of this evidence, however. Support comes from an unexpected source when PC Quinnan discovers some damning evidence from Santini's past: this is not the first time that Santini has been accused of harassment.

Fox transfers out of Sun Hill due to Santini.

Quinnan warns Santini to back off.

Main: **Ackland, Stamp and Garfield prevent Quinnan from getting physical with the increasingly dodgy Santini.**

'Urgent Assistance' 15 SEPTEMBER 1998
written by Steve Griffiths directed by Albert Barber

Wound up by PC Hollis's implication that PC Hagen is a swifter area car driver than he is, driver PC Stamp responds immediately, with his colleagues PCs Ashton and Quinnan, to a call for assistance from PC Page. Taking a short cut down a narrow one-way street his way is suddenly blocked by a van. Losing patience, he reverses at high speed back down the street and, despite a shouted warning from his passenger Quinnan, he crashes with a sickening thud into a pedestrian.

The pedestrian, Simon Attwell, later dies in hospital, and the shocked Stamp faces a criminal investigation. He is suspended from driving until the trial for causing death by dangerous driving. Rumour soon spreads around the station that he was racing Hagen to the scene of the crime at the time of the accident. Increasingly frustrated at not being able to get behind the wheel to investigate calls that come in, and with the court case hanging over him, Stamp finds the pressure on him soon starts to take its toll.

'Taking Sides' 22 SEPTEMBER 1998
written by Len Collin directed by Tania Diez

PC Stamp attends the funeral of Simon Attwell, the accident victim, to pay his respects, but is confronted by Attwell's girlfriend Jane. She accuses him of harassment and removes his offering of flowers from the grave.

Worry over the case has a knock-on effect as PC Quinnan confides his concern to PC Garfield that he will be asked to testify for the prosecution at Stamp's trial.

Things go from bad to worse for the already irritable Stamp. Arresting a chauffeur for driving a stolen car, he manages to ruin a bride's big day. Finally, he discovers that Attwell's girlfriend has made a formal complaint about him to Inspector Monroe.

As a mark of respect, PC Stamp lays flowers at the grave of the accident victim.

Top left: **Stamp copes badly when returned to area car duty following the accident, only to be paired with rival driver Hagen.**
Left and bottom left: **A stuntman rehearses the accident in which PC Stamp runs down a pedestrian.**
Below: **Behind the scenes: a make-up artist at work.**

'Deadly Impact' 29 SEPTEMBER 1998
written by Anthony Valentine directed by Ged Maguire

It is the day of Stamp's trial for causing death by dangerous driving. He is painfully aware that he could be given a ten-year sentence if things go badly for him. PCs Ashton and Quinnan also attend court: Ashton as witness for the defence and Quinnan as witness for the prosecution. Quinnan is dismayed at having to give evidence against his long-time colleague, while Ashton becomes increasingly agitated over how to present his version of events. Chief Inspector Conway saves the day when he quietly takes Ashton aside and tells him not to be nervous – if he just does his best to look after his fellow officers he will always have a clear conscience.

Stamp is found not guilty of the original charge, but is fined for the lesser charge of driving without due care and attention. However, before the relief can begin to set in, he is handed a letter informing him that he will now have to appear before a police disciplinary board.

'Big Day' 6 OCTOBER 1998

written by Nicholas McInnerny and Carolyn Sally Jones
directed by Marcus White

It is a day of celebration for Chief Inspector Conway and DS Beech who are called to Police HQ in Hendon to receive their Long Service and Good Conduct Medals. PC Stamp, meanwhile, is wracked with nerves as he faces his internal disciplinary hearing.

At the award ceremony, Beech bumps into an old flame, DS Sue Heywood. She is working with the police internal investigation team, looking into the affairs of a colleague suspected of taking bribes. This news comes as a shock to Beech as he realises the investigation could uncover the fact that in the past he too received a hefty bribe from a gangster. In the process of making sure that his secret remains safe, he is able to reflect on his career, and heed the warning.

Confronting the possibility of the end of his career, Stamp nearly loses his nerve completely – even walking out of the hearing at one point. It is PC Garfield who forces him to confront his own particular personal demons and return to face the board. Stamp is eventually reinstated.

Top: **Christopher Timothy plays a detective suspected of taking bribes, but if he goes down, Beech does not intend to go down with him.**
Bottom: **At the enquiry PC Stamp i cleared of causing death by dangerous driving.**

'Making Up' 13 OCTOBER 1998
written by Chris McWaters directed by Brian Parker

While PCs Stamp and Quinnan are out on patrol, Stamp notices a red Fiat following their car. Although at first he tries to ignore it, he is eventually forced to try to question the mystery driver. As he approaches the car on foot, the driver accelerates towards him.

Having tried to put the trauma of the accident, court case and disciplinary hearing behind him and concentrate on his job, on doing a Police National Computer check on the car's registration Stamp is horrified to discover that the Fiat belongs to Simon Attwell's girlfriend.

Meanwhile, PC Hagen goes undercover as a prostitute in the Sun Hill cells in a bid to catch solicitor Richard Kemp-Jones, who is suspected of dealing in fake passports. Though she gains the solicitor's trust, the set-up begins to unravel during a CID interview in which, in an attempt to entrap Kemp-Jones, he is shown fake photographic evidence of a drug deal which he quickly recognises as such. Thinking on his feet, DI Deakin saves the day by making up a story that they have another witness statement – finally causing the smug Kemp-Jones to trip himself up.

PC Hagen working undercover as a prostitute.

On her first appearance in The Bill, DC Holmes crosses with 'Robocop' DS Boulton.

'The Cross' 20 OCTOBER 1998
written by Maxwell Young directed by Ian White

It is the first day at Sun Hill for DC Holmes, and things do not start well when she is asked to partner the station's most difficult detective, DS Boulton. Boulton is on the trail of two men who used a forged cheque to buy a motorbike – the cheque could link them to a building society robbery. Holmes fails to endear herself to Boulton when she arrives late for an arrest and then, to her dismay, is knocked to the ground by an escaping suspect. She partially redeems herself by getting the suspect's vehicle registration number, but Boulton is not impressed and makes it abundantly clear by his aggressive manner.

Although the two men escape, Holmes discovers that the getaway car belongs to a man who has form for armed robbery. This links them to information about a major drugs deal at a club involving the same criminals. CID officers and the Drugs Squad begin a raid. Undercover inside the club, Holmes and Harker arrest a suspect for dealing in cocaine, but police back-up are prevented from entering by the club's burly security guards. By the time the police gain entry, all the cocaine has vanished.

'Cast No Shadow' 27 OCTOBER 1998

written by Steve Griffiths directed by Chris Lovett

DS Boulton and DC Carver are called to investigate the attempted abduction of fifteen-year-old Leanne Adams on her way home from school.

The girl's father, a brewery boss, tells CID that he has been approached by organised criminals wanting to take over the licence of a pub that was closed down due to an arson attack. When he refused to comply, they threatened his family. The man is frightened and requests protection for his family, and names the ring-leader as Michael Hyde. Intelligence suggests that Hyde is linked with a number of criminal gangs in the north. When Boulton comes up with a connection in Manchester, DCI Meadows gives Boulton and Carver the go-ahead to follow him there.

Information is hard to come by and soon the two are ensconced in a pub, mulling things over. Their London accents soon draw attention, and a gang of young men are spoiling for a fight. A booming voice from across the bar orders the youths to stop. Carver spins around at the sound of a familiar voice, and to his astonishment discovers it is his ex-boss, Frank Burnside.

Things appear to have changed for Burnside, and as the Sun Hill officers become more involved in the search for and arrest of Hyde they begin to wonder which side of the law Frank is on.

Top: **On an undercover investigation in Manchester, Boulton and Carver turn up more than they expected.**
Bottom: **A disapproving Sgt Cryer books Burnside into the cells.**

'Betrayal' 29 OCTOBER 1998
written by Tony Mulholland
directed by Chris Lovett

DS Boulton and DC Carver escort a subdued Burnside back to Sun Hill in handcuffs. As they leave the train, Burnside narrowly escapes a shot from a hitman's gun.

Suspicion hangs heavily in the air as Sgt Cryer books in Burnside, warily taking him to a cell. Convinced Burnside is bent, DCI Meadows takes his time granting an audience. But it is soon confirmed by Scotland Yard that 'none of this is as it seems'. Burnside has been working on an important undercover operation, reporting directly to an Assistant Commissioner at the Yard. Meadows and his team have egg on their faces.

Burnside's target is a Croatian heroin importer named Kurvec, and the Sun Hill pursuit of linked villain Hyde has endangered not only his operation, but also his life. Despite doubts higher up — including the deep suspicions of Meadows — Burnside elects to return to the fray and, it transpires, to rekindle an affair with Hyde's wife.

Top: **Burnside's lover wrestles for control of the gun.**
Bottom: **In rehearsal, Burnside pleads for his life.**

'All For One' 30 OCTOBER 1998
written by Edward Canfor-Dumas directed by Delyth Thomas

Resident bad boy PC Santini is called to the scene of an accident involving a lorry and a car, resulting in the car dangling precariously over the river bank with the semi-conscious and badly injured driver still at the wheel.

On arrival, Santini discovers that the fire brigade has yet to show up and that the car is rocking dangerously. The driver regains consciousness sufficiently to ask Santini to tell his wife and kids he loves them. Meanwhile, PC Harker arrives and together he and Santini attempt to secure the car with rope – Santini heroically leaping into the water in an effort to wrap the rope around the vehicle. The injured driver takes the opportunity to beg him in confidence to remove a present for his mistress from his pocket – a package of cocaine.

Despite their best efforts, when the other emergency services arrive the paramedics declare the man dead. Santini is left in the uncomfortable position of needing to keep his promise without arousing suspicion. He removes the packet from the man's personal effects at the mortuary, but an assistant has already seen it. Colleagues do not know whether to consider Santini a hero or a problem.

In an emergency, Santini radios for back-up.

'Trial Run' 3 NOVEMBER 1998
written by Patrick Melanaphy directed by Dominic Lees

Thrusting young DC Skase is tempted by the offer of easy money to moonlight as a bodyguard. At first he is told he will be escorting a gorgeous model to a photo shoot, but there is a change of plan and he finds himself on a shopping trip with the two teenage sons of a wealthy Middle-Eastern businessman. But at least he is driving a shiny new Mercedes.

Unfortunately, once the boys are away from their father they undergo a personality change. Ahmed is rude and arrogant, Mahan is sullen and disgruntled. They bicker constantly. While in an expensive shop, Skase is persuaded to try on an extortionately priced jacket – only to find that while he has been preoccupied Ahmed has taken the keys and driven off in the Mercedes.

Skase has a terrible day, chasing Ahmed to his girlfriend's exclusive apartment where a party is taking place. The guest list includes drug dealers who are in turn being pursued by Boulton. By the skin of his teeth, Skase gets the dreadful brothers to the airport in time to catch their flight, but concludes that moonlighting as bodyguard to the rich and famous is not so glamorous after all – he would rather stick to the day job.

Bodyguard boss Peterson tears a strip off a defiant Skase, who has lost the company Mercedes.

'Section F' 6 NOVEMBER 1998
written by Richard Stoneman   directed by Chris Hodson

A promotion opportunity gives rise to competition between two ambitious applicants, Chief Inspector Conway and DCI Meadows. Both believe that Chief Superintendent Brownlow is the key to their promotion and, to his embarrassment, both vie for his support.

Things go wrong for them when the Area Inspection Team tour Sun Hill. Meadows has enlisted the help of Skase to ensure that all is ship-shape for the visit, but he is unaware that PCs Garfield and Quinnan are deliberately setting up practical jokes – such as removing chairs meant for the inspectors – in revenge for Skase having sold Quinnan a duff car. Conway, meticulous about custody procedure, attempts to make sure that all runs smoothly in that department. But his efficiency ends in spectacular slapstick fashion when a prisoner pulls a basin off the wall and floods the entire cell area.

When a report comes in of an escaped prisoner being in the Sun Hill area, Conway seizes the chance to go out and make an arrest. In his eagerness he fails to call for back-up, and encounters a desperate man with a gun. It is more by luck than judgement that he manages to resolve the situation.

'Bad Chemistry' 10 NOVEMBER 1998
written by Maxwell Young directed by Rob Evans

DC Holmes is surprised when the victim of what looks like a domestic assault refuses to press charges against her assailant.

Although the woman gives a statement at Sun Hill, she almost immediately wants to retract it when a tough-looking young man called Steve Hastings comes to collect her from the station. Light begins to dawn when DCI Meadows is informed by DS Lockyer from Merseyside Drugs Squad that Hastings is a target under surveillance for a major amphetamines investigation and that this arrest has compromised their operation.

Lockyer summons Holmes and surprises her with the news that her abuse victim is in fact married to Hastings, and berates her for interfering in a petty domestic abuse case. Holmes attempts to put matters right by involving CID with the drugs squad, and sharing a tip-off that Hastings could be setting up a deal.

However, all does not go to plan when an elaborate surveillance of what they think is a drugs factory fails to deliver a suspect or any major drugs trawl.

Top: **DS Daly and DC Holmes look for evidence in a major amphetamines investigation.**
Above: **Actress Joy Brook, who plays DC Kerry Holmes, rehearses on location.**

'Dog Eat Dog' 13 NOVEMBER 1998

written by Rod Lewis
directed by Phillipa Langdale

When a teenage prostitute is admitted to hospital with knife wounds Sgt Cryer is appalled by PC Santini's flippant attitude to the crime, and his unorthodox method of detection.

Cryer questions a friend of the victim, another prostitute, who says that she was recently threatened by a similar-looking knifeman who demanded money from her. Meanwhile, Santini is out with PC McCann at the scene of the crime searching for witnesses. It is Santini who finds that a recently released prisoner named Morton fits the man's description.

At St Hugh's Hospital, PC Page is just about to get some co-operation from the victim, when two young villains – who are known to the police for drug dealing – stroll in. The sight of them scares the girl into silence. It seems that the two villains have moved on from supplying drugs to running girls, and they are not happy that one of their employees has been knifed.

Santini tells Cryer that it is a shame the two young pimps cannot be told where Morton is, thereby saving the police the trouble of dealing with him. Santini pays a late visit to a pool hall frequented by the villains and, before leaving, surreptitiously deliberately drops hints as to where Morton can be found.

Shortly after, Morton is found by PC Page lying on the floor of his bed-sit, covered in blood, with multiple stab wounds.

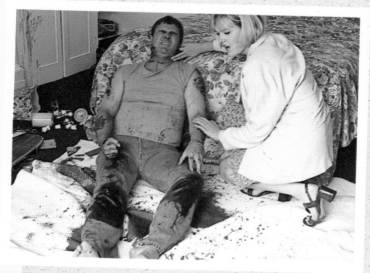

Top: **PC Page's prime suspect, Morton, is found with severe knife wounds – an attack indirectly sparked by Santini's attitude problem.**
Bottom: **Deakin, Beech and Cryer question Morton to discover the identity of his assailants.**

'Indiscretion' 17 NOVEMBER 1998
written by Arthur Ellis directed by Derek Lister

Investigating a fire at a sex cinema club, CID are appalled to discover a collection of videotapes of children giving evidence in abuse trials – all copied from the Metropolitan Child Protection Team (CPT) originals.

At the club, DC Skase speaks to the club manager, who has been injured in the fire, who says that he refused entry to regular customer Eric Chable because he was drunk. Chable later returned to douse the place in petrol and set fire to it, setting himself on fire in the process. Chable is now in hospital, but a search of his car reveals an unlabelled video cassette.

When CID view the video they find that it is a CPT tape showing thirteen-year-old Gail Werral giving evidence. DCI Meadows suggests that Chable might have been running off copies of these tapes and selling them. But as the CPT is the direct source for such evidence, there must be a direct link. DI Deakin instructs CID officers to tread carefully.

Skase questions Chable in hospital and discovers that the tape is six years old, and Gail is now Chable's fiancée. Chable burnt down the club because he found two men watching the tape. It emerges that the club's owner has a conviction for importing and processing child pornography. It is DC Rawton who eventually discovers the leak stems from a weak link at a solicitor's office.

'The Rate for the Job' 20 NOVEMBER 1998
written by J.C. Wilsher directed by Frank Smith

DS Daly is on the trail of a wanted 'fence' called Hanway, who is only too conscious of Daly's interest in him. Daly comes close to nabbing Hanway, but an observation set-up goes wrong and no more money is available for surveillance work. The matter is further complicated by the involvement of DS Beech, who is approached by an old flame, Veronica, now Hanway's girlfriend, who offers him a £3,000 bribe for information on Daly's investigation.

Their differing policing methods bring Beech and Daly into open conflict. Daly says he would never bend the rules to set up a criminal, but Beech has no such qualms. DCI Meadows, however, thinks that using Veronica to try to set up Hanway is worth a try, and agrees to let Beech handle the case as long as he is partnered by a watchful DS Boulton.

When Beech is offered a bribe for information on DS Daly's investigation, how will he respond?

'For Interest Only' 24 NOVEMBER 1998
written by Don Webb directed by John Bruce

A local journalist digs up an old story about the now Chief Superintendent Brownlow failing to recover jewellery stolen twenty years ago in a burglary at a country house. When the journalist requests an interview, Brownlow is not best pleased to be reminded of this blot on his record.

Ray Catton, the burglar who committed the crime but never revealed the whereabouts of the loot, is currently in prison for shooting dead two villains – for no apparent reason. Thinking it might be worth looking into the case again, Brownlow goes to the prison to visit.

Subsequently, Catton has a heart attack. Lennox talks to Catton's brother and discovers that the men he killed had threatened his daughter Elaine when she was a child, and had sent him her nail clippings and her photograph to show that they could get close to her. Catton's heart attack, Brownlow learns, has been brought on by the receipt of fresh threats made to Elaine and her children. Now Catton will reveal the location of the stolen jewellery in exchange for the protection of his family.

'The Fat Lady Sings' 27 NOVEMBER 1998
written by Richard Stoneman
directed by Robert Del Maestro

While investigating a burglary at a very expensive block of riverside flats, PCs Stamp and Page are taken aback to meet Sun Hill's new DC Lennox, who lives there in some style.

Lennox's colleagues are also surprised to discover that the new DC seems to know everyone who's anyone socially – from DCI Meadows to a judge and his wife who visit the station to complain about threatening letters they have been receiving. Gossip abounds at Sun Hill, but PC Page is left red-faced when she finds out that it is Lennox's wife, with her high-flying job in the City, who is responsible for the couple's lifestyle.

Lennox becomes involved in the case involving the judge. It turns out to be connected to a case that PC Quinnan is investigating, in which an amateur opera singer has been receiving strange phone calls from a man recently released from a prison where she performed in a visiting production of *Sweeney Todd*. It is Lennox who notices the link between the two cases – one of the letters sent to Judge Pinter contains a quotation from *Sweeney Todd*.

Gossip is rife at Sun Hill when Lennox arrives and clearly enjoys a wealthy lifestyle.

'Too Many Cooks' 1 DECEMBER 1998
written by Nigel Baldwin directed by James Cellan Jones

At a charity lunch, Chief Superintendent Brownlow is introduced to businessman Paul Chambers and his daughter Carol, the hotel's chef. Shortly after, Carol goes missing.

CID officers check the hotel's CCTV video, and one of them recognises a local drug dealer talking to Carol. When the dealer is brought in for questioning and confronted with the video, he admits Carol bought cocaine from him but claims she was then approached by two Chinese men who took her away.

It transpires that she has been kidnapped by a Triad gang who rent a property from Carol's father that they are using as a brothel and a receiving house for illegal immigrants. Chambers's wife confesses to Brownlow that she thinks her daughter has been kidnapped as a warning to prevent her husband from informing the authorities about their activities. Brownlow takes over the case, insisting on a raid to resolve matters and free Carol, despite the danger to her life that path engenders.

Brownlow interviews the concerned parents of a kidnap victim who has been abducted by a Triad gang.

'Team Play' 4 DECEMBER 1998

written by Anthony Valentine   directed by Gwennan Sage

At Hilton Road nurses' home PCs Hagen and Garfield attempt to calm a distraught nurse who has been attacked. It seems that this is not the first attack at the home. In CID, DCs Lennox and Proctor eagerly vie to lead the investigation. But it is Lennox who gets the case when he manages to slip out of an officer safety training course he is supposed to be attending, by claiming he has already done it.

DCI Meadows insists that the somewhat burly and patently unfit Lennox at least attend the refresher course. Even in the warm-up session, Lennox finds it hard to keep up. In addition, to Meadows's extreme chagrin, Lennox manages to spend most of the day rushing off to the nurses' home to interview witnesses.

Eventually, a positive identification is made against a window cleaner called Gerry, who is found to possess a cupboard full of stolen women's underwear ...

'Heat and Light' 8 DECEMBER 1998

written by Gregory Evans   directed by Ged Maguire

A newly converted block of flats, Carpenter's Court, has recently been the scene of a fire. DS Boulton, who is investigating a spate of arson attacks, meets a fire investigator who tells him that this latest fire is the arsonist's most ambitious yet.

When DS Boulton and DC Holmes interview the firefighters they mention Adam Mars, a young man who likes to hang around the brigade and watch them do their job. Boulton thinks they have their man and arrests Mars, who immediately confesses to the fire.

However, a visiting offender profiler, DS Hunt, disagrees with Boulton's verdict, believing that as the latest fire is a much more sophisticated arson attack than the others it must have been set by someone with more technical knowledge. She explains that arsonists often take the credit for fires they have not started. The fire investigator concludes that the fire might actually have been set by a firefighter.

'Ticking Clocks' 10 DECEMBER 1998

written by Gregory Evans   directed by Barbara Rennie

A new-born baby has gone missing from St Hugh's Hospital. The only lead that PCs Ashton and Hagen can find is a nurse who saw a woman in a doctor's coat heading towards reception carrying a baby.

The case is passed on to CID. DS Boulton and DC Holmes visit the teenage mother of the baby who finds it difficult to remember precise details about the abduction and refuses to name the father. With little to go on, Boulton suggests consulting profiler DS Hunt, but is disappointed to learn she is unavailable. On an impulse Boulton drives to Bramshill Police College and persuades her to help.

Meanwhile, DI Deakin speaks to a classmate of the teenage girl and discovers that the father of the baby is their teacher. When questioned, the teacher reveals that his wife is unable to conceive, but quashes the idea that she took the baby. It is DS Hunt who recovers the baby by helping the mother to recall details of the abduction, encouraging her to make a television plea, and profiling the abductor. In the course of this process, Hunt becomes emotionally involved with both the case and DS Boulton.

Offender profiler DS Hunt takes a shine to handsome DS Boulton.

'Strange Bedfellows' 11 DECEMBER 1998
written by Len Collin directed by Frank Smith

Convicted child molester Carl Jones is brought in to Sun Hill promising information on paedophile rings in return for a safe house. He is further tempted by early parole if he can name the members of the 'Circle of Friends', a paedophile ring he once belonged to, and lead the police to the body of a schoolboy believed to have been murdered by the gang. Despite the fact that they do not always see eye to eye, DCIs Meadows and Burnside join forces, finding that they have a common purpose when confronting the horrors of a paedophile ring.

Jones, however, gives Burnside and DC Lennox the runaround, pointing them towards lock-up garages that have long since been demolished, and saying he did not know the other gang members as they used code names. An angry Burnside eventually makes the decision to bring Jones face to face with the murdered boy's parents in order to shock him into revealing the truth.

'Live and Ticking' 15 DECEMBER 1998
written by Candy Denman directed by Peter Cregeen

As PC Hollis walks past a phone box near a park a teenage boy shouts at him to get clear, just as the box explodes, throwing him to the ground. Later, at St Hugh's Hospital, though superficially unharmed Hollis claims to be suffering from shell shock.

Meanwhile, there has been another explosion, this time at a primary school. Inspector Monroe calls in the Bomb Squad who think the device was made by amateurs. PC Garfield arrives at the school to find a ten-year-old boy with a severe hand injury. Another pupil claims that the injured boy had a bomb made out of bits of pipe and nails which he took from under his brother's bed. On investigation it becomes clear that the injured boy's brother has made ten bombs which he has sold on to friends. The friends have no idea of the danger they are in.

Chief Inspector Conway suggests publicising the problem of the remaining devices and declaring an amnesty to get people to come forward, but Chief Superintendent Brownlow disagrees with his strategy. However, it is Conway who eventually resolves the situation by sticking to his guns and advising the schoolboys of an amnesty against his superior officer's wishes. Thanks to Conway, all the homemade bombs are recovered and, though the schoolboys escape prosecution, they have learned a severe lesson.

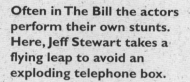

Often in The Bill the actors perform their own stunts. Here, Jeff Stewart takes a flying leap to avoid an exploding telephone box.

'All The Lonely People' 17 DECEMBER 1998
written by Tony Mulholland directed by Delyth Thomas

When Mary Sloane is found dead and two more women go missing in similar circumstances, DC Rawton goes undercover as a 'lonely heart', placing an ad in the local press to try and catch the man responsible. But after five tedious dates, Rawton seems no nearer to finding the right man. A meeting with one promising possibility, Drake, ends abruptly when the waiter fails to identify him as the man who met Sloane. However another date, Freeman, is positively identified by the waiter.

DCI Meadows interviews Freeman, who admits having dinner with one of the missing women, but insists he left her at a coffee shop. Both Freeman and Drake leave messages asking Rawton out again. She is not sure whether to accept, but fellow officers looking into the case suggest there could be more than one killer at large.

One of the missing women turns up, and it is discovered that the other was killed by a jealous husband. Finally it is Drake who reveals himself as Sloane's murderer when he invites Rawton to see a Bruce Lee film – Sloane had a ticket stub from a Lee film in her pocket when she was found.

'The Personal Touch' 18 DECEMBER 1998
written by Patrick Melanaphy directed by Ian White

When the house of gangland boss Jimmy Smith is ransacked by burglars and his girlfriend, Melanie, is attacked by the same violent gang, he contacts his old friend DS Beech and promises him a familiar backhander if he can help trace the assailants. Having taken a £20,000 bung from Smith earlier in the year, after managing to get him off a charge on a technicality, Beech is in a position to be pressurised by Smith.

The matter is further complicated by the arrival in Sun Hill of DCI Burnside on the trail of the same gang. Burnside warns Smith about taking matters into his own hands but the gangster is not easily intimidated. Beech is the one losing sleep, his corrupt past now in danger of exposure by Burnside.

Then the focus of the investigation turns to Melanie, and it emerges that she has a much more intimate knowledge of her attackers than she has so far admitted. She has had a secret relationship with Smith's rival and her love letters proving the liaison are stolen during the burglary. Melanie is now being blackmailed.

In 'The Personal Touch', like is pitted against like: gangster against gangster; Beech against Burnside.

Above: **DC Jim Carver and DCI Frank Burnside lead the fight against gangland crime.**
Right, top: **Gangster Jimmy Smith, played by Leslie Grantham, offers DS Beech money in return for information.**
Right, bottom: **Despite Beech's efforts to keep him out of the investigation, Burnside starts to smell a rat.**

'Time Gentlemen Please'

21 DECEMBER 1998
written by Ray Brooking
directed by Albert Barber

Under DS Daly's supervision, CID set up an undercover operation to trap a pub protection gang. Daly poses as the landlord of the Askil Arms, with DC Rawton pulling pints as his 'wife'. DC Skase plays the jovial barman, while downstairs in the cellar DC Carver is manning the covert videos and microphones set up to catch the gang.

The pub is awash with dodgy drinkers, rowdy lads and small time dealers in cigarettes from hijacked lorries, but by early afternoon there are still no gang members operating a protection racket. However, at the end of the day Carl White, a nineteen-year-old who has already been pointed out to the Sun Hill team as a cannabis dealer, staggers through the door badly bruised and bleeding and falls unconscious to the floor.

Carver's cameras have failed to pick up the assault, but two burly regulars are immediate suspects and CID soon find them providing the lead they need.

DC Daly and DS Rawton pull pints in the hope of pulling down a major pub protection racket.

'Puzzled'   22 DECEMBER 1998

written by Ben Cooper   directed by Steve Shill

Hollis organises a pub quiz between Sun Hill and Barton Street to raise money for his police caravan. Meanwhile, when PC Quinnan reluctantly takes his mother's cat to the vet he becomes involved in a major drugs investigation. An unconscious dog has been brought in which the vet recognises has been injected with heroin.

Quinnan is horrified to learn that sadistic brothers Mehmet and Kemal Laza have been released from prison and are menacing the dog's owners, Ian and Danny. However, when he arrives at Ian's flat to ascertain the facts of the case, Ian takes one look at the uniform and makes a run for it, sending the elephant statue he is carrying crashing to the ground. The statue shatters to reveal bags of uncut heroin.

Ian tells CID that he and Danny smuggled the drugs back from Thailand for the Lazas, but that the brothers would not pay them for the drugs. When Danny is kidnapped, Boulton uses Ian to trap the Lazas. The operation is successful, and the officer joins the pub quiz to find Barton Street cheating. Hollis does a deal with them and manages to raise some extra cash for his caravan.

'Christmas Star' 24 DECEMBER 1998
written by Terry Hodgkinson directed by Tom Cotter

When a twelve-year-old girl is badly injured in a hit-and-run accident on a zebra-crossing, PC Santini is determined to nail the driver.

Thanks to a witness who took the car's registration number, the police discover that the black BMW belongs to a man called Beattie who has a record for drunk driving. But Beattie has by this time reported the car stolen, and claims he was not driving it at the time of the accident. Though Beattie fails a breathalyser test the police do not have enough evidence to hold him. When Santini informs the child's father he is devastated.

The difficult Santini shows a softer side of his character when he visits the accident victim in hospital, discovers she is an Arsenal fan and vows he will get one of the team to visit her as a Christmas present. PC Page bets him £20 that he will never manage it, but she is stunned when French striker Emmanuel Petit walks through the hospital doors with a big bunch of flowers for Laura.

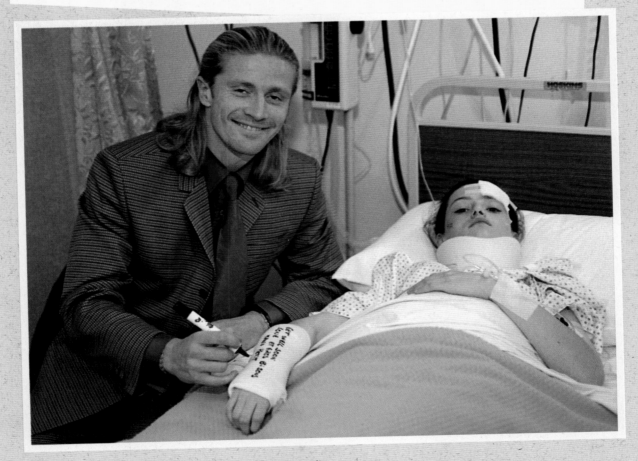

Arsenal striker and star of France's 1998 World Cup winning team Emmanuel Petit visits a young hit-and-run victim in hospital.

'S.A.D.' 31 DECEMBER 1998
written by Chris Jury
directed by Chris Hodson

Officers at Sun Hill are yawning over a tedious post-Christmas shift until they are jolted out of their apathy by a succession of events which send them lurching into chaos. From the discovery of an unconscious pensioner to the report of a burglary, followed by a brawl in a pub, the pace is unforgiving.

PCs Quinnan and Santini investigate the pub brawl and are bemused to discover a heavily pregnant woman attacking her husband, who insists on pressing charges against her for GBH.

Once at the station PC Garfield finds himself choking on his mince pies as he attempts to police the woman's five young hyperactive sons. Chief Superintendent Brownlow is not amused by their antics. Meanwhile the mother goes into labour in her cell, and a pile-up on the motorway means that no ambulance can get through. It falls to poor Brownlow to spring into action with his first-aid book – while Boyden and Ackland look on, clueless – and deliver the sixth young menace!

A chaotic day in Sun Hill culminates in members of the squad pulling together to deliver a baby in a cell.

The Sun Hill squad congratulate the reconciled happy couple.

'Long Term Investment' 5 JANUARY 1999
written by David G. McDonagh directed by Jonathan Campbell

Sun Hill CID hope they can resolve the last part of an investigation when an old adversary, Frank Tully, is released from prison and tries to retrieve the £30,000 ransom money he was paid – but never collected – from the kidnapping of a young girl. Tully and his associate Hackett were both convicted eight years ago, each insisting that the other had hidden the money. On his release, Frank Tully is kept under observation by DI Deakin and his fellow officers in the hope that he will lead them to the money. Now that both he and Hackett are free, DCI Meadows hopes the cash will materialise.

When Hackett tips off the police that Tully is to open a security deposit box containing the money the next day, Deakin and DS Beech watch on security cameras. But the box is empty save for a gun which Tully suddenly points at Hackett, demanding to know where the money is.

'Chasing Shadows' 14 JANUARY 1999
written by Alan Pollock directed by Herbert Wise

The Konya Turkish coffee shop is under observation, suspected of being an illegal gambling den. Large sums of money are changing hands, but the Sun Hill squad need to know exactly how the café owner takes his cut.

The Drugs Squad provides an officer, Senyuz, a Turkish national, to visit the café undercover. He reports to Sgt Boyden that the scam revolves around the punters paying £50 for a £1 cup of coffee – effectively their entrance money for a game.

Boyden decides to raid the café, and the owner is arrested for illegal gambling. But, later, when Senyuz fails to turn up for a meeting, it is feared that he has been abducted. As the investigation progresses and a connection with a Turkish drug smuggling ring is revealed, CID unwittingly gatecrash a similar operation run by the Drugs Squad and DCI Meadows is faced with the dilemma of compromising the entire operation in order to save Senyuz's life.

'Follow Through' 21 JANUARY 1999
written by Steve Handley directed by Tom Cotter

A massive rise in the use of heroin at Newington Prison for women has lead to an increase in violence. When a prisoner receives a savage beating and DS Daly's enquires get nowhere, DC Kerry Holmes faces the toughest assignment of her career to date when she is sent in undercover to smash a drugs ring.

DS Daly has convinced Holmes to pose as a prisoner doing five years for drug smuggling. But inside no one trusts her, and she soon gets into a fight during a basketball match, finds herself sexually propositioned by a fellow prisoner in the showers, and that the prison officers treat her like dirt.

Back at Sun Hill, DC Skase is enjoying Holmes's predicament, much to the distaste of a concerned DC Lennox; but with Holmes's help Daly is beginning to get some results and she determines to see the job through. Holmes shows the men in CID in no uncertain terms that she is tough enough to survive life inside and obtain the evidence required.

'Walking on Water'
26 JANUARY 1999
written by Graham Mitchell
directed by Chris Lovett

When a drugs raid goes wrong, there is suspicion that someone from Sun Hill has leaked details. The blame lies with DCI Meadows's team, and he is forced to defend his people fiercely against the Drugs Squad's allegations.

Bad feelings between DS Daly and DS Beech reach boiling point when Daly suspects that Beech is responsible for the leaks. The straight-dealing Daly believes Beech has gone too far this time, and sets out to prove his colleague is taking bribes from gangsters. An explosive confrontation follows as the horrified Beech realises that Daly is getting close to finding out the truth — culminating in a shouting match and Beech pushing a shocked Daly into the canal.

In a risky operation, DC Holmes goes undercover as a prison inmate to crack a drugs ring involving the prison officers and inmates.

'The Wrong Horse' 28 JANUARY 1999

written by Stephen Plaice   directed by Brian Farnham

For a change, PCs Hagen and Garfield spend a weekend in plain clothes, at the races. They are to protect Irish jockey Terry McCaul who is a key witness in a betting ring trial. The case involves the doping of a favourite horse, and a suspicious bookie, Barney Grimmond, who has made threats to McCaul to stop him testifying.

With McCaul racing the next day, Garfield and Hagen keep an eye on him over the weekend at a country house hotel near the course. But Hagen becomes alarmed at the amorous attention she is attracting from McCaul, and is put out when someone tries her door in the middle of the night. But McCaul is fast asleep in another room and Hagen spots a silver Jaguar driving off.

As the race nears its climax the next day, McCaul suddenly falls from his horse, dislocating his shoulder and putting himself out of action. Hagen begins to realise that the drugs ring is bigger than they have supposed, and that McCaul is not as innocent as he seems.

Top and right: **A weekend at the races? Garfield and Hagen get lucky when they're assigned to protect a witness.**

'No Love Lost' 2 FEBRUARY 1999

written by Katherine Way   directed by Albert Barber

At a night club, self-styled ladies' man and resident charmer Sgt Boyden boasts to PCs Ashton and Santini that he can pick up any girl he chooses. With what his colleagues think is the luck of the devil, Boyden is approached by an attractive young woman, Natalie, and soon whisks her back to his place.

The following morning, Boyden is called to an assault in the road where Natalie lives, and questions a woman whose husband has been hit with a whiskey bottle. Natalie suddenly appears and it transpires that she is the woman's daughter. She is only fifteen years old.

Things get worse when a neighbour tells Boyden that the mother is a prostitute, and that her two daughters are mixed up in the same lifestyle. Natalie asks for Boyden's help but he is too scared to give it, fearing his night with the girl will be revealed. As the investigation goes wrong – with the revelation that Natalie's stepfather has been prostituting both her and her sister, and with the police caught in the family's web of lies – Natalie, desperately unhappy with her lifestyle, kills herself.

Boastful Boyden bites off more than he can chew when a one-night stand with an attractive young student threatens to turn into an underage sex scandal.

'Pond Life' 4 FEBRUARY 1999

written by Matthew Leys directed by Tim Holloway

A convicted paedophile, Ballantyne, is released from prison to be placed in a 'safe house' in Sun Hill. DCI Meadows and DC Rawton meet him at the train station and take him to a sparsely furnished council house. Meadows wants his whereabouts kept quiet.

However, a local paper gets hold of the story and publishes the details, including the location of the house. Soon a small crowd gathers outside and 'child molester' is sprayed on the front door. On the door step, PC Quinnan finds himself pelted with eggs following a woman's outburst that her ten-year-old son has not yet returned home from school, and that a man fitting Ballantyne's description was seen talking to him outside the school gates.

When a major disturbance takes place outside the house, the police are forced to give in to the crowd and move Ballantyne. The missing boy, it transpires, has simply run away. He is later returned to his mother, safe and sound.

Realising that he will allways get the blame regardless of his innocence, a devastated Ballantyne hangs himself.

Tempers run high when the safe house address of a convicted sex offender is revealed in the press. The police bow to public opinion in order to protect the paedophile.

Stamp and Garfield keep a watchful eye on the volatile crowd.

'Murder, What Murder?' 9 FEBRUARY 1999
written by Terry Hodgkinson directed by Derek Lister

When a headless corpse is fished out of the River Thames, it is believed that a suicide has been decapitated by a passing boat.. However, Garfield is soon distracted from his enquiries by attractive local journalist Carrie Winkler, whose interest in him is more than just professional.

Winkler shows Garfield a hidden video camera trained on a car park that she discovered in her newspaper's archive; but, in doing so, inadvertently blows a long-term police surveillance operation. The camera was being used to catch a big-time bullion robber. However, with the identification of the body in the river it becomes clear that there is a link between the two crimes. Garfield finds out that the identity of the drowned man – a small-time villain whom no one has missed – is being used by a much bigger villain, Zweibel, to cover his tracks.

When the head is found it is concluded that it was severed after the man drowned in order to prevent easy identification. The investigation becomes a murder enquiry. Zweibel is now the prime suspect. When Winkler hopes to sweep Garfield off to France for a romantic weekend, she is thwarted by the demands of the investigation. But they are soon reprieved – Zweibel has already escaped the law and departed for Spain.

Top: **The Sun Hill Chronicle journalist turns up evidence linking the dead body to another crime.**
Left: **Local reporter Carrie Winkler assists PC Garfield in his investigation.**

'Age of Chivalry' 11 FEBRUARY 1999
written by Simon Moss directed by Steve Shill

A bedraggled young woman, Bennet, reports her rape to PCs Stamp and Garfield, and is comforted at Sun Hill by specially trained PC Page. Bennet explains that she was grabbed by two men as she left the tube station and driven to a wasteland, and that one of the men told her he had seen her in a local wine bar earlier that evening.

When police take her to the wine bar, she is shocked to see the man who raped her working as a waiter. He is soon under arrest, but claims to have been in a cinema at the time of the crime. His father tells the police of his son's work colleague, Watkins, who frequently gives him lifts. Watkins is brought in for questioning and his car linked to the attack.

To everyone's surprise DCI Burnside, well known for his view that rapists are the lowest form of scum, decides to let him go. Irritatingly, Burnside will only tell his colleagues that 'like God, he moves in mysterious ways'.

Burnside's action causes a chain of events in which the two suspects, attempting to destroy evidence, incriminate themselves and are arrested. But the victim is not amused by Burnside's irreverent method of investigation and ends up feeling humiliated, despite the successful arrest of her attackers.

'Slinging Mud' 18 FEBRUARY 1999
written by David Hoskins directed by Harry Bradbeer

DCI Meadows finds himself accused of corruption when he gets a rare chance to send down notorious drugs villain Frankie Leicester. But Leicester fights dirty: as well as intimidating witnesses, he conspires to make Sun Hill CID look corrupt.

Meadows believes the evidence of key witness Anna will be enough to convict the dealer, but Leicester has arranged for his defence lawyer to submit new evidence that Meadows has taken bungs and set up a bank account for the money. But although a furious Meadows denies the accusations, he finds it difficult to explain away the £5,000 in cash that is discovered under a desk in CID, and how his personal details have been used to set up a new bank account.

Rumours begin to circulate at Sun Hill, and Meadows becomes seriously worried about his own liberty. With the assistance of a concerned DI Deakin, Meadows manages to turn the situation to his advantage and save his reputation.

'Under Duress' 23 FEBRUARY 1999

written by Dale Overton directed by David Moore

The fire service alert DS Boulton to some sinister secrets about a recently burned-out house – bars and locks point to its use as a prison.

When a Ukranian girl is picked up for shop lifting, she reveals to DC Rawton that she, along with several other East European girls, has been forced into prostitution and made to take drugs. The girl is now terrified that she and the other girls will be killed by their captors for causing the fire.

DC Rawton decides to do some investigating on her own. But when she returns to the burned-out house she is herself kidnapped by a vicious pimp called Ursin. Handcuffed, she is driven to a deserted industrial unit where some of the girls are already locked up. Things look bleak for Rawton, especially when Ursin threatens to inject her with heroin. Having posed as a client to find out the truth, Boulton arrives in the nick of time to rescue Rawton and the other girls, and to arrest Ursin.

'Sleeping With The Enemy'

25 FEBRUARY 1999

written by Anthony Valentine directed by Jo Johnson

At an upmarket hotel, DCI Burnside is hot on the trail of a predatory gang of women promising sex to businessmen, then stealing from their rooms. A businessman has complained to the hotel manager about his credit cards being taken. As soon as Burnside sees CCTV footage of the man drinking with a woman at the bar he realises what is going on and who is responsible – Victoria is a known prostitute and an old adversary of the DCI.

At the hotel's next business convention, DCs Skase and Lennox check in under false names. But they take their role a little too seriously, and Skase is soon seducing one of the delegates, while Lennox is invited back for a nightcap by a beautiful woman. But Lennox is knocked out when his drink is laced, and Skase is gutted to find that he has missed the target and picked up a bonafide saleswoman instead.

Burnside finally manages to trap the two-woman team by posing as a businessman himself and entrapping one of them. Burnside and Victoria share some fond memories of the last time they met before he escorts her down to the station.

**Burnside gets to grips with a high-class call girl played by Glynis Barber in a guest appearance…
…and *Right*, recognises an old adversary in a prostitute played by Lorraine Chase.**

PC Quinnan collars youths responsible for turning over a flat, and radios for assistance.

'Badlands' 2 MARCH 1999
written by Scott Cherry directed by Nick Laughland

CID, led by 'Robocop' DS Boulton, are after two sadistic burglars who are attacking pensioners by dousing them in petrol and threatening to set them alight, before ransacking their homes.

Boulton is about to take a much-needed break when he hears of a new lead. He cancels his plans and, to the consternation of his already alienated colleagues, embarks on an obsessive drive to catch the perpetrators. Acting on a hunch that the man behind the crimes is Mick Glover, a crook with form for burglary, he determines to raid Glover's flat. But Uniform have had the flat under observation for six weeks and fear their operation will be scuppered by Boulton's actions. Ignoring his colleagues' advice, and the concerns of Uniform, Boulton nevertheless goes ahead with his raid … and finds nothing.

The disastrous raid puts PCs Quinnan and Garfield's informant Janie in fear of her life. Answering a call-out to Janie's flat on the local estate, the two PCs find her flat smashed up and covered in graffiti. Quinnan goes after the suspects, only to find himself in the estate youth club surrounded by fifteen young men who savagely assault him while he screams for assistance over the radio. Garfield, trapped outside, can only watch in horror.

'Eyes Everywhere' 4 MARCH 1999
written by Neil Clarke directed by Ian White

While PC Quinnan remains in a critical condition in St Hugh's Hospital intensive care, suffering from a severe beating and a stab wound, his colleagues search the estate where he was attacked in the hope of finding the youths responsible. But residents are too scared to come forward with any information and their enquiries are met only with silence.

As PC Garfield saw the attack on Quinnan, he manages to identify a good number of the gang and the squad conduct a house-to-house search to bring them in. When a young member of the gang, Kevin White, is brought in for questioning he is clearly in fear of the others, but slowly begins to open up and tell them about the so-called 'Sun Hill Massive'.

The shell-shocked Garfield is furious with DS Boulton when he attempts to shift responsibility for the attack on to Quinnan himself by claiming that Quinnan should have been wearing a protective vest. Bad feelings escalate and, when Garfield discovers that Boulton did not have authorisation for the raid, Sgt Boyden has to break up the ensuing fight.

It is only when the Sun Hill team, acting on a tip-off, raid Glover's flat again that they are able to solve the burglaries and arrest Glover's son Ben together with Kevin White for the assault on and stabbing of PC Quinnan. As they are brought into custody, Sgt Cryer receives a message from the hospital and announces to all units that Quinnan is out of danger.

Sgt Boyden is forced to separate two warring officers when Boulton has the temerity to suggest that the attack on Quinnan was his own fault.

'Yesterday's Hero' 18 MARCH 1999
written by Len Collin directed by Delyth Thomas

DS Boulton is running a surveillance operation on a man called Maltese Joe. Working together with PCs Hollis and Garfield he is hoping to catch Joe selling drugs from his grocery stall.

Due to continued ill-feeling between Boulton and Garfield, however, all does not go smoothly. Boulton's continued goading about the attack on PC Quinnan is more than Garfield can take. He finally explodes, head-butting Boulton and almost breaking his nose. Boulton does not report the incident, and denies there is any problem between them.

Meanwhile, Quinnan is recovering in hospital, but becomes increasingly irritable and bored. His out-of-hours visitors and special treatment stoke the resentment of a fellow patient, Gary Jukes, who is also in hospital following a stabbing. Jukes claims the police did nothing about the crime committed against him. Quinnan determines to help Jukes but, as he learns more, he finds that the facts do not fit together. The sad truth emerges that Jukes's stab wounds were self-inflicted – he was trying to attract the pity of his wife, who threw him out when she found him in bed with another man and will not let him see his young son.

Boulton and Garfield are uneasily reconciled when Hollis helps Garfield to realise that his continued rage is due to his feelings of impotence at watching Quinnan suffer and being unable to help.

Delyth Thomas puts actor Peter Ellis through his paces.

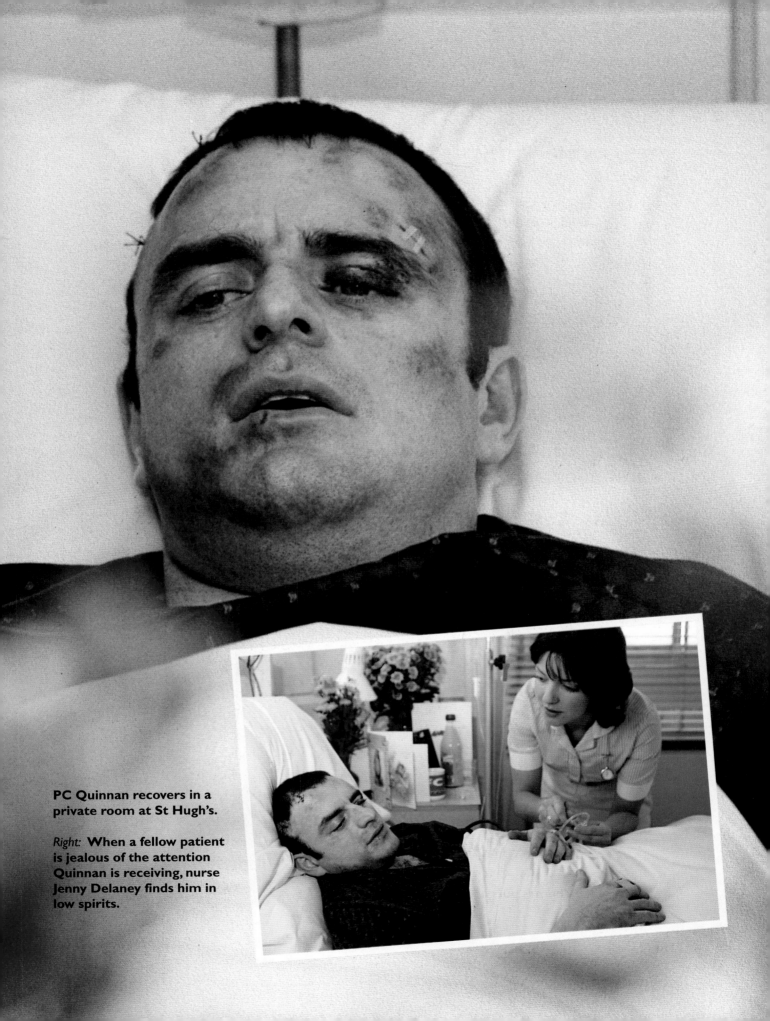

PC Quinnan recovers in a private room at St Hugh's.

Right: When a fellow patient is jealous of the attention Quinnan is receiving, nurse Jenny Delaney finds him in low spirits.

A career move? Chief Inspector Conway hosts a police spot on local radio.

'On Air' 23 MARCH 1999

written by Len Collin directed by Brian Farnham

A madman who attacks women in their homes at night is terrifying the female population of Sun Hill. PCs Hagen and Santini are called to a help a distraught woman who has been held captive by a man who smashed a glass lamp in his hand and dripped the blood onto her night-dress. There have been a number of similar cases in the past six months so, in desperation, CID enlist the help of a local radio station to try to coax their man into the open.

Chief Inspector Conway takes to the airwaves, appealing for information during an interview with a local DJ. A mystery caller says he cannot stop what he is doing – but his number can only be traced to a mobile phone. Conway makes a breakthrough when he dubs the man 'The Creep' and receives an angry response. When a previous victim joins the radio appeal to tell her story, 'The Creep' takes another woman hostage and subjects her to a terrifying ordeal live 'on air' until the Sun Hill squad track him down.

Tommy Boyd plays popular DJ Steve Mason, who hits on the idea of making an appeal for witnesses on air.

'To Catch A Cobra' 25 MARCH 1999

written by Manjit Singh directed by Tom Cotter

Sun Hill's toughest twosome, DCI Burnside and DS Boulton, join forces in pursuit of Burnside's slippery old adversaries the Roy brothers. The Roys are suspected of masterminding the theft of precious gems from a museum collection of Indian items from the colonial era.

It is soon discovered that Amit and Atul Roy are also trafficking in illegal immigrants. When officers begin to see that a number of other crimes in Sun Hill link back to the brothers, Meadows suggest they all team up. But Boulton takes co-operation a bit too far. Aping Burnside's 'no nonsense' style of detective work, he uses an underage informant to get information he requires.

'Weekends Are For Wimps'

30 MARCH 1999
written by Nigel Baldwin
directed by Jo Shoop

When DCI Meadows phones in sick one Saturday, Chief Inspector Conway is forced to miss the Chelsea football match that he has tickets to.

DC Lennox questions a drunk driver arrested by PC Santini, and discovers it is the same man they have been seeking in connection with a series of armed robberies. Now the man has been caught, Meadows renews his interest in the job and gets up from his sick bed to do the interview – much to Conway's annoyance.

Meanwhile, a disturbance is going on in the station as Sgt Cryer tries to prevent a woman from attacking former Chief Inspector Pavey and his wife, claiming that they have kidnapped her husband, Alan Bird. Bird has a long criminal record, but when Conway hears about the incident he is soon unravelling the dark connection between the chief inspector – who was once his hero and mentor – and the criminal past of Bird.

Top: **Sgt Cryer and PC Harker deal with a disturbance outside Chief Inspector Pavey's house.**
Bottom: **Actors Eric Richard and Matthew Crompton run through a segment in which they shoot off to the scene of the crime.**

'Piggy in the Middle' 1 APRIL 1999
written by Clive Dawson directed by Brian Parker

Frank Burnside returns to Sun Hill to investigate an arson attack, only to discover that it is part of a terrifying witness intimidation campaign.

On patrol, PC Ashton sees two men preparing to firebomb a family home, but they speed off in a waiting car before he can confront them. In CID, Burnside thinks it bears all the hallmarks of another recent attack. One of the family has a criminal record and, via his underworld contacts, Burnside discovers that the attack was meant to frighten a sister-in-law who is soon to give evidence in the trial of a man accused of stabbing a crack cocaine dealer. She now refuses to testify.

This is the second of two witnesses who have been frightened into withdrawing their evidence, and DC Holmes is left as the only remaining witness for the prosecution.

Holmes too becomes a target for intimidation, and is subjected to a terrible ordeal when she climbs into her car outside a pub and is set upon by two masked men wielding baseball bats. Fortunately it is only the car that is badly damaged, but the attack fires her determination to catch the villains and, together with Burnside, she does exactly that.

'Sex, Lies and Videotape' 6 APRIL 1999
written by Tony Mulholland directed by Paul Murton

Chief Superintendent Brownlow allows a documentary film crew to record the day-to-day police work at Sun Hill, as it seems like a good public relations exercise. But trouble begins when most of the officers cannot help playing up to the cameras.

Headed by Jane, a video-journalist, the documentary crew film an observation on a local drug dealer and the ensuing raid on his house, including Boulton's violent arrest of a suspect he erroneously believes is in possession of a gun. Boulton is furious when he discovers that Jane has filmed him. Brownlow becomes increasingly concerned as Jane tries to make her material more dramatic and begins to capture things on film that do not follow the good PR line he envisaged.

Meanwhile, Sgt Boyden has to sort out a war between prostitutes and local residents. He nearly comes unstuck when one of the prostitutes produces a video of herself having sex with a policeman and threatens to hand it to the documentary maker if their rights are not upheld. But, by covertly filming Jane offering him money, Boulton saves the day and Brownlow triumphs admirably in what could have been a tricky situation.

Brownlow valiantly attempts to mediate at a meeting between prostitutes and local residents.

'Out and About' 8 APRIL 1999

written by Richard Stoneman
directed by Pip Broughton

For the first time since the vicious attack in which he was stabbed by a gang of youths, PC Quinnan bravely returns to life on the beat at Sun Hill. But he finds it harder than he had anticipated.

Chief Superintendent Brownlow wants to start him off on light office work, but Quinnan is adamant that he should go out on patrol. And so, despite doubts as to his fitness for the job Quinnan is sent out on patrol in an area car with PC Stamp.

Soon Quinnan's nervous state of mind is affecting his judgement. When the officers spot some youths breaking a car window, they give chase. But despite being told to split up, Quinnan follows Stamp and says it would be better for them to stick close together. When they do catch one of the youths Quinnan is convinced that he has got a knife and gets rough – but, after a search, finds nothing.

When a call comes through to deliver a death message, Quinnan meets a Gulf War veteran whose traumatic experiences match his own and realises that he still has not come to terms with the attack. However, Sgt Boyden saves the day when he persuades Quinnan to accompany the squad on a raid that night as a way of gaining credibility with his colleagues again. Quinnan saves PC Hagan from a heavy-handed thug and finds his confidence restored.

On the raid, PCs
McCann and Garfield
restrain and arrest a
suspected drug dealer.

On PC Quinnan's first
day back at the job
following the attack,
Boyden takes him on a
drugs raid to jolt him
back into action.

'Kiss Chase' 13 APRIL 1999
written by Maxwell Young directed by Dominic Lees

When a teenage girl, Abby, who is the central witness in a domestic violence case, becomes obsessed with handsome young PC Luke Ashton it seems at first that he is playing the bad guy. However, when she accuses him of getting her pregnant her emotions become increasingly unstable, putting both the court trial and Ashton's career in jeopardy.

Abby is due to testify against her stepfather, who is accused of assaulting her mother and breaking her fingers. But her emotional state leads her to come apart under cross-examination and contradict her own statement.

Ashton reports to Sgt Cryer that it is impossible he could be the father of the baby, and Cryer suggests he make an official complaint. But all does not look good when Ashton eventually admits to Chief Inspector Conway that he did sleep with the girl, but used protection.

In the end it is Abby's attempted suicide which prompts the revelation that it is her violent step-father who is responsible for her pregnancy.

Gossip is rife when PC Ashton is accused of getting a teenage witness pregnant.

'On The Road' 15 APRIL 1999
written by Chris Ould directed by Audrey Cooke

In an off-beat episode, DCs Lennox and Rawton drive to Salisbury to pick up Riordan, a prisoner who has conned a woman out of £50,000. On the journey back to Sun Hill both DCs learn a salutary lesson on the thin line between reality and fiction and how a confidence game is set up from the prisoner who is clearly an old pro, not to mention an old rogue.

When their car overheats and Lennox is forced to pull into a service station, Riordan first cons money out of Lennox by sleight of hand and then absconds. Neither detective really knows what is going on. They are simply left clutching a left-luggage receipt for Waterloo station.

At the station the £50,000 is recovered, together with a mysterious note for Stella, the woman whom Riordan conned out of her savings. When Stella arrives at Sun Hill to identify her property, and Riordan makes a surprise reappearance, the two are reunited and claim to be in love. Both Lennox and Rawton are left with the sceptical feeling that it is they who have been conned.

'Pressure Point' 20 APRIL 1999
written by Rod Beacham   directed by Brian Parker

DCs Lennox and Proctor have been called to a woman's house: she has been burgled while out at her daughter's wedding. Her living room is littered with the debris of stolen wedding gifts.

Having recently read an article explaining that earprints are as distinctive as fingerprints, Lennox is delighted when he has the place dusted for prints and finds an earprint on the window. Despite the fact that juries are sceptical about the new technique, he finds a suspect and hopes to use the new knowledge to scare him into a confession.

Meanwhile, Proctor interviews the reticent witness of an assault which links in with the case, and thinks he can impress his colleagues. However the woman will not testify as she was at her lover's flat at the time of the incident and does not want her wealthy and influential husband to find out. DI Deakin encourages Proctor to get tough, and eventually he achieves significant results – the woman's lover is arrested, but Proctor probes further to find that the rich husband could be responsible for a whole spate of crimes.

'Look Away Now' 22 APRIL 1999
written by Michael Jenner   directed by James Cellan Jones

Sun Hill officers including PC Harker, DS Beech and Sgt Boyden all have their own reasons for pursuing a local thug, but have to deal with the neighbours from hell when they help the local council target an anti-social family – the Drakes – who are suspected of drug dealing.

Harker talks to one of the neighbours, who claims that one of the Drakes broke into his house, stole a credit card from his post and took £2,000 from his account. Harker confronts and arrests Drake – but the complaining neighbour later finds a sinister funeral wreath delivered to his doorstep, and withdraws his complaint. The police are left wondering whether the Drakes' hold on the estate is simply too strong.

Blinded by science, DC Lennox is determined to use new earprint technology to catch a crook.

Celebrity Appearances

The Bill has no trouble enticing top stars into intriguing roles in hard-hitting stories about prostitution, drugs, or the criminal underworld. With the show's broad, enduring appeal, many well-known actors from stage and screen are dedicated viewers themselves and vie for the chance to play an old rogue, like Ronald Pickup in an episode entitled 'On the Road', or a gangland boss, like Leslie Grantham in 'The Personal Touch', in which his girlfriend played by Denise Van Outen is attacked by a violent gang of burglars.

Casting director Lisa Harris explains that there used to be a rule banning famous faces from The Bill. When Michelle Collins and Patsy Palmer appeared, it was *before* they were well known. Happily all that has changed and Harris is casting stars like Rik Mayall, Tommy Boyd, Hugh Laurie, Christopher Timothy, Lorraine Chase, Glynis Barber, Nigel Planer and, most recently, The Who's Roger Daltrey, an old friend of Billy Murray since they both appeared in *McVicar*.

In an episode robustly entitled 'Sucking Eggs', Liz Smith plays grandmother Edna Finch, who appears, to an initially sympathetic Beech, to be a little old lady robbed of all her worldly possessions, whilst all the time dealing in little white tablets.

In the three-part story 'Humpty Dumpty', Rik Mayall plays hapless gambler turned murderer Patrick Massie. Here he is arrested for shoving his sixteen-year-old homeless son Jimmy off a high rooftop. Jimmy had witnessed his father in a fatal tussle with wealthy drunk Bannerman, and had to be silenced.

Former Spandau Ballet popstar turned EastEnders most-wanted man, Martin Kemp takes a break to run amok at Sun Hill as out-of-control gunman Tom Marsh, in an episode called 'The Bus Driver's Prayer'.

Background: **Hugh Lawrie, for once not trying to make us laugh, guest stars as defence council over three episodes entitled 'Good faith'.**